Transferring Information Literacy Practices

Billy Tak Hoi Leung · Jingzhen Xie ·
Linlin Geng · Priscilla Nga Ian Pun

Transferring Information Literacy Practices

上海交通大學出版社
SHANGHAI JIAO TONG UNIVERSITY PRESS

Springer

Billy Tak Hoi Leung
University of Macau Library
Macau, China

Jingzhen Xie
University of Macau Library
Macau, China

Linlin Geng
University of Macau Library
Macau, China

Priscilla Nga Ian Pun
University of Macau Library
Macau, China

ISBN 978-981-13-7742-6 ISBN 978-981-13-7743-3 (eBook)
https://doi.org/10.1007/978-981-13-7743-3

Jointly published with Shanghai Jiao Tong University Press, Shanghai, China
The print edition is not for sale in Mainland of China. Customers from Mainland of China please order the print book from: Shanghai Jiao Tong University Press.

This Springer imprint is published by the registered company Springer Nature Singapore Pte Ltd.
The registered company address is: 152 Beach Road, #21-01/04 Gateway East, Singapore 189721, Singapore

Foreword

Information literacy is an ability to use information technology, to acquire information, to evaluate information, and to use the knowledge gained in a person's study, work, and everyday life. An information literate person not only knows where to acquire information but also how to evaluate and use information effectively and creatively. Nowadays, more and more jobs are related to information technology and its application. Information literacy has become indispensable in life and career development. Teachers or students, managers or staff, all need these skills to succeed and thrive in modern society.

Anthony Comper, a Canadian banker, told the 1999 Commerce graduating class at the University of Toronto that information literacy is essential to future success. He said: "Whatever else you bring to the twenty-first century workplace, however great your technical skills and however attractive your attitude and however deep your commitment to excellence, the bottom line is that to be successful, you need to acquire a high level of information literacy."[1]

Here, two points need to be emphasized: effectively and creatively. In Chinese, Huo yong. Huo means effective and creative, yong means use and apply, to put what you have learned into practice. To get information is not so difficult, but to effectively find and creatively use information is the basis of information literacy.

An information literacy program is more than library use. It lays emphasis on the whole process of information management, from acquisition and cataloguing of information to analysis and synthesis, for problem-solving purposes. Therefore, information literacy goes well beyond accessing information. Being information literate leads you to new knowledge, new discoveries and success in sifting through the complexities of our digital age.

The library is the perfect place to acquire and practice these skills. You can benefit greatly from such study and practice at the University of Macau Library, where a team of four experienced reference librarians are available to give lectures,

[1] Rockman, I. (2004). Introduction: The importance of information literacy. In I. R. Associates (Ed.), Integrating information literacy into the higher education curriculum: Practical models for transformation (p. 8). San Francisco: Jossey-Bass.

provide research reports, and meet your ongoing needs as you learn and develop information literacy. This textbook draws on their successful careers in this field, as well as their teaching and practical experiences.

Macau, China
February 2019

Dr. Wu Jianzhong
University Librarian
University of Macau

Acknowledgements

The writers of this book, the staff from the University of Macau Library, express warm thanks to Prof. Kimberly Hughes, Associate Professor in Applied Linguistics in the Department of English, Faculty of Arts and Humanities, UM for providing detailed editing and helpful comments to prepare this manuscript for publication. She was our first editor of the book, and we thank her for her support and valuable contribution, especially under time pressures.

Immense gratitude to Mr. Stephen Chong Meng Lei, Functional Head of the Library Systems and Information Technology Unit, University of Macau Library. Special thanks to Peiying Liu, Deputy Editor-in-Chief at the Oriental Publishing Center, China Publishing Group Corp. for her guidance and assistance.

Thanks also go to Xiaofei Li, Editor at the Shanghai Jiao Tong University Press, for contributing to the publication.

The authors appreciate Prof. Ruhua Huang, Professor in Information Management at Wuhan University, for her support of this project.

Contents

Chapter 1
Information Literacy for Life

Abstract How our country deals wirealities of the information age will have enormous impact on our democratic way of life and on our nation's ability to compete internationally. Within America's information society, there also exists the potential of addressing many long-standing social and economic inequities. To reap such benefits, people as individuals and as a nation must be information literate (ACRL 1989). In this first chapter of the book, we explore what information is, what information literacy is, what constitutes information literacy skills, and why information literacy is important.

1.1 Information

What is information? "Information" is not just facts, but rather selecting useful data and that analysis is needed to do so. Paul Zurkowski, proponent of the concept of information literacy, considers that "information is not knowledge. It is concepts or ideas which enter a person's field of perception, are evaluated and assimilated, reinforcing or changing an individual's concept of reality and/or ability to act" (Zurkowski 1974, p. 1). Information is "in the mind of the user." It enhances one's ability, but only after it is evaluated and absorbed. Information has the following intrinsic characteristics:

(1) Useful information spreads knowledge;
(2) Information is objective. It is everywhere and could be everything: a statement, a fact or an object;
(3) Information is useful, but its usefulness is contextual. Specific information has a specific audience;
(4) The usefulness of information is reflected through analysis and evaluation. Typically, there is a lot of information about a particular subject, as well as many sources and forms of that information. Only through effective analysis and evaluation can we extract reliable, useful and time-sensitive information tuned to our target audience.

B. T. H. Leung et al., *Transferring Information Literacy Practices*,
https://doi.org/10.1007/978-981-13-7743-3_1

1.1.1 Types and Forms of Information

Information can be divided into factual information and analytical information. Factual information points to objective facts. For instance, it is a fact that Isaac Newton, an English mathematician and famous physicist, was born in 1643 and died in 1727. Factual information provides a unique, unchanging answer. Analytical information involves interpretation of factual information, explaining its meaning and impact or telling why it is important or relevant. This involves information literacy, knowing what is relevant and how it is useful. For example, Macao had a total population of 656,700 at the end of March 2018 marking an increase of 3,600 quarterly, compared to the previous year. The female population (348,100) accounted for 53.0% of the total population (Statistics and Census Service Macao 2018). What is important is knowing that the population is increasing and knowing that over half the population is female. That information is obtained through analysis and comparison of facts, so statistical knowledge and analytical skills are required.

Objective information is based on facts, synthesizing information from different sources. You may need to present the different sides of an issue and show how it can be understood from different perspectives. Objective information can be found in sources such as reference books, impartial media reports, encyclopedias and textbooks. We must be aware that not all information is objective, however. Some of it is biased, or subjective, communicating personal viewpoints, opinions, interpretations or judgments. News reporting typically relies on objective information. Subjective information may also be reported, but from a particular perspective—opinions, assumptions, interpretations and beliefs expressed by individuals, groups, organizations, editorials, reviews, blogs, biographies, comments on the Internet, and so on.

Another consideration is whether the information is reliable or fake information. Unbiased information based on facts is reliable. Fake information is made up or outright lies. Fake news on the Internet and social media is widespread, so knowing if a source is objective and reliable is very important when relying on digital information. Digital information is provided by the web, social media, databases, etc., whereas physical information exists in actual books, magazines, newspapers, and the like.

Information having academic value is particularly important for scholars and students, as it tends to be much more reliable than popular information, which can be fake. Academic literature usually has the following characteristics:

(1) It has been peer reviewed (experts in the field have "judged" it and considered it worthy of publication);
(2) The author's name, institution and contact information are provided;
(3) Research methods and research results are clearly explained;
(4) A summary abstract is provided and references are cited.

Academic integrity is observed. College students and serious scholars must understand what academic literature is, where to find it and how to use it in your discipline or specialty area.

Another way to look at information is how well it provides direct evidence. Primary sources are the first-hand information, original records created at the time historical events occurred or right after the events took place. Memoirs, diaries, manuscripts, letters, interviews, photos, government information, first-time news reports and objects or artefacts are examples of primary sources. Secondary sources are created based on the analysis, evaluation and interpretation of a particular historical event. Secondary sources are usually in the form of commentaries and criticisms based on someone's analysis or interpretation of primary information. Scholarly books and research articles are good examples of this type of analysis. The distinction between primary sources and secondary sources often depends on how they are used. For example, a literary analysis of Eileen Chang's novels written in the 1930s was a secondary source at the time this analysis was accomplished. It becomes a primary source when, in 2019, a scholar wants to study criticisms of Chang's novels before 1949.

Sources that synthesize, list or describe materials from primary sources and secondary sources are considered tertiary sources. Tertiary sources are usually not credited to a specific author. Reference books, bibliographies, encyclopedias, indexes, almanacs, directories, and resource discovery tools are examples of tertiary sources. Please realize that, while primary, secondary and tertiary information have different purposes and values, all are important resources for academic research.

When most of us think of information, we think of it existing in written form, but audio is another important channel for acquiring information. Lectures, meetings, oral communication, and recordings are all forms of audio communication. Visual information is provided in pictures, charts, graphics, videos, and so on. Users need to select and consider the most relevant, reliable, credible and useful information for your research needs, whether it be print, audio, visual and in all its forms/media.

1.1.2 Information Resources

When you use the library, resources are generally divided into print resources or electronic resources. Both are important in your research. Digital resources are becoming more and more common and present numerous advantages in terms of information access and dissemination. However, physical resources are vital and cannot be ignored. An information literate person knows how to use and evaluate different forms of information resources in order to meet their task and scholarly needs.

Many students like to rely on digital information because it is freely available online and convenient to retrieve and use. It covers a wide range of subjects, but most of it is non-academic and the creators and disseminators of the information are unknown, not experts, and may possibly even be paid to create fake information.

Beware of relying too much on digital, nonacademic sources when you analyze and evaluate information.

The library is still the best place to obtain abundant, reliable and up-to-date information. Public libraries provide information for everyone. Universities and research libraries have unique advantages in providing academic information and supporting scholarly research. Knowing how to use library resources is central to information literacy and paves the way to your academic success.

1.1.3 Information Discovery

Since so much information is available, much of it in digital form, information discovery tools are crucially important when finding and selecting the most useful and relevant information for your research needs. Library catalogs, databases, and information discovery tools must be used knowledgeably and efficiently.

In the late twentieth century, more and more user-friendly databases were developed, making readers increasingly independent and self-confident if they know how best to use information discovery tools, or information and communication technologies (ICTs).

1.2 Information and Communication Technologies

However, it is important to understand that information literacy is not the skills of using information and communications and technologies.

1.2.1 What Are Information and Communication Technologies

According to the definition put forward by UNESCO (2007), the term "information and communication technologies" (ICTs) refers to "forms of technology that are used to transmit, process, store, create, display, share or exchange information by electronic means. This broad definition of ICTs included such technologies as radio, television, video, DVD, telephone (both fixed line and mobile phones), satellite systems, and computer and network hardware and software, as well as the equipment and services associated with these technologies, such as videoconferencing, e-mail and blogs." ICTs are technologies that provide access to information through telecommunications. In addition to the technologies and the associated equipment and services, ICTs also include the Internet, wireless networks, cell phones, smart phones and other communication mediums.

ICTs literacy is a key attribute for everyone. Acquiring ICTs skills is essential for learners in the twenty-first century because only by acquiring the necessary ICTs skills will they be able to understand, actively participate in, and fully benefit as a member of the information society and the knowledge economy (Farmer and Henri 2008, p. 18). The application of ICTs promotes learning, brings innovation to teaching and has significantly changed the way information is collected and used. For example, ICTs are good for promoting resource-based learning and teaching activities with purposes of solving problems. ICTs help to achieve high quality education, which is particularly significant in less developed countries.

1.2.2 Information and Communication Technologies Skills Are Not Information Literacy

ICTs skills enable individuals to effectively communicate in the information age. However, ICTs literacy is not the same as information literacy. Information literacy is broader, deeper and more complex than ICTs literacy. For example, information literacy comprises seven core abilities, as follows: (i) identify an information need, (ii) assess current knowledge and identify gaps, (iii) construct strategies for locating information, (iv) locate and access information needed, (v) review the research process and evaluate information, (vi) organize information in a professional and ethical way and (vii) apply knowledge acquired (SCONUL 1999).

Information literacy is more than practical use. It is crucially associated with pedagogy and is a process of learning how to learn and thus an ability of knowing how to learn. The famous SCONUL model was reviewed and revised in 2011 and reviewed again in 2015 to reflect this. Another example is that the Association of College and Research Libraries (ACRL) adopted the *Framework for Information Literacy for Higher Education* on January 11, 2016 to replace the *Information Literacy Competency Standards for Higher Education of 2000. The framework focuses on the foundational ideas of information and information literacy in response to the rapidly evolving higher education environment and the dynamic and often uncertain information ecosystem. The revisions of information literacy standards and frameworks* further reveal the differences between information literacy and ICTs literacy.

1.3 Information Literacy

Information literacy is a key asset for the twenty-first century learners. Information literate people "know how to find, evaluate, and use information effectively to solve a particular problem or make a decision—whether the information they select comes from a computer, a book, a government agency, a film, or any number of other possible resources" (ACRL 1989). Information literacy is associated with active learning, reflective thinking/critical thinking and knowledge application.

1.3.1 Redefining Information Literacy

Because the way information is created, located, used and disseminated has undergone profound changes, information literacy has been redefined. In early 2016, ACRL adopted the new *Framework for Information Literacy for Higher Education* and expanded the scope of information literacy to metaliteracy, which indicates an overarching set of information abilities. The framework formulated the following new concept of information literacy: "Information literacy is the set of integrated abilities encompassing the reflective discovery of information, the understanding of how information is produced and valued, and the use of information in creating new knowledge and participating ethically in communities of learning."

Along with traditional information skills such as determining, accessing, locating, understanding, producing and using information, collaboration in information production and information sharing is also an important literacy skill. Lifelong learning, critical thinking and ability of ongoing adaptation to the new information world are also considered as the essential skills of information literacy.

The *Framework for Information Literacy for Higher Education* (ACRL 2016) also specifies the following six concepts:

(1) Authority is constructed and contextual;
(2) Information creation as a process;
(3) Information has value;
(4) Research as inquiry;
(5) Scholarship as conversation;
(6) Searching as strategic exploration.

This framework emphasizes the fundamental ideas of information, highlights critical thinking, and stresses lifelong learning. A significant message transmitted by the framework is that, with information acquisition becoming relatively easy, the skills for locating information are still important, but critical thinking, information ethics, and lifelong learning have also become the essential information skills to acquire.

1.4 Importance of Information Literacy

Early in 1982, the futurist John Naisbitt, wrote in his book *Megatrends* that "we are drowning in information but starved for knowledge" (Naisbitt 1982). The twenty-first century is, particularly, an age characterized by information explosion and technological advances. It is critical to know how to locate, identify and use information wisely and effectively to fulfill study, work and daily-life purposes. Students should not be drowned in information, but know how to use information to make good decisions. Information literacy helps in regard and thus is an essential life skill to acquire in the twenty-first century.

1.4.1 Independent and Lifelong Learners

The information society is a learning society where earning is no longer limited to the classroom nor entirely relies on the guidance of the teacher. Learning takes place throughout a person's life and on a voluntary basis. Information literacy, deeply connected to and promoting lifelong learning, enables a person to meet his information needs throughout his life.

1.4.2 Skilled Researchers

Information resources are abundant in the information age. Most of the time, compared to the previous generations students know how to use information discovery tools, but are not always better prepared for research. Information literacy teaches students how to become good information analyzers and researchers. Without information literacy skills, it is hard for a student to achieve his academic and social learning goals.

1.4.3 Responsible Citizens

Seeking and using information has become a basic human right and behavior. Information literacy constitutes the basest set of skills and concepts that every citizen must attain in order to be functionally competent. A fundamental requirement for being a responsible citizen is to be information literate.

In short, students are the future of the society. They need to be a good information user and information creator and is able to successfully participate in collaborative spaces in order to succeed in and better serve the world of the twenty-first century. Thus, the importance of information literacy skills is reflected in this fact that they help a student to become an independent and lifelong learner, a skilled research and a responsible citizen.

1.5 Features of This Book

The purpose of this book is to teach library readers how to acquire information literacy in the information age. The first part (Chap. 1) is an introduction, reviewing information and information literacy. The second part (Chaps. 2–7) describes search strategies, how to use different methods to find information, and introduces the topic content search, including searching for relevant information in the fields of the humanities, social sciences, medical science, and science and technology, etc. The third part (Chaps. 8–9) is about how to evaluate the literature, through some useful tools for document collation, assessment and analysis. Through systematic learning, learners must have the ability to be literate.

These capabilities include understanding where and how to find library and network resources, the characteristics of the literature or information, and learning to use a variety of tools, such as library catalog retrieval, data collection, sorting, analysis, evaluation and other techniques. The acquisition of these abilities is also a learning process. Therefore, libraries organize different types of learning activities, including workshops, lectures, and university courses to help library readers achieve the best learning outcomes. Library readers have the ability to master information literacy, which will be of great benefit to their life, work, study and research, and will be used for lifelong.

Today's technological development also makes knowledge exist in different media. It is not only an entity book, but an e-book, a database, a sound material or a video, etc., which becomes complicated. In terms of content, readers should learn how to distinguish between true and false, good and bad, different points of view and perspectives, and even the content of the organization, analysis and evaluation must have the ability of information literacy.

As library readers, they face the vast sea of knowledge. In today's information society, they become helpless. They need the skills of information literacy to use libraries and network resources effectively. This book assists readers in solving this problem.

1.6 Summaries of the Book Chapters

Chapter 1 Information Literacy for Life

This first chapter of the book explores what information is, what information literacy is, what constitutes information literacy skills, and why information literacy is important.

Chapter 2 Information Search Strategies

This chapter introduces some commonly-used search strategies that can help improve your efficiency when finding useful information. These search strategies are applicable in all search tools and databases, with a few variations from one database to another. It is recommended that you read the "Help" section in each database before searching for the first time in a new database.

Chapter 3 Resource Discovery Tools and Multi-disciplinary Databases

This chapter introduces the two most commonly used tools for academic resource retrieval, resource discovery services and multidisciplinary databases. You can use it as the first entry point in your research to find trusted and relevant resources.

Chapter 4 Information Literacy General Resources, Tools and How to Access Them

This chapter introduces the print and electronic general resources and tools for each discipline in the University of Macau Library and how to access and use them.

Chapter 5 Information Literacy Resources in Science

This chapter is intended to help health science, medicine, engineering and information technology students quickly locate resources and reliable internet resources related to your study and research.

Chapter 6 Information Literacy Resources in Social Science

This chapter is intended to help arts and humanities, business and management, education, law and social science students quickly locate resources and reliable internet resources related to your study and research.

Chapter 7 Search Engine

Search engines are designed to help people find information stored on the Internet. They enable users to find needed information across billions of web pages with relatively little efforts. This chapter introduces the types of search engines and the reuse of Chinese and Western search engines.

Chapter 8 Developing Information Literacy Skills with Various Tools

This chapter introduces a number of selected commonly used tools for supporting and enhancing information literacy, namely search tools, online surveys and questionnaires tools, citation analysis tools, bibliographic management tools, as well as plagiarism and similarity checkers.

Chapter 9 Assessment of Learning Outcomes for Information Literacy

This chapter discusses about the importance, process, methods and instruments of assessment for information literacy. It gives a guidance on assessing information literacy from using standards to integrating framework into a learning environment.

References

ACRL (1989) Presidential Committee on information literacy: final report. http://www.ala.org/acrl/publications/whitepapers/presidential. Accessed 15 Oct 2018

ACRL (2016) Framework for information literacy for higher education. http://www.ala.org/acrl/standards/ilframework. Accessed 15 Oct 2018

Farmer LS, Henri J (2008) Information literacy assessment in K-12 settings. Scarecrow Press, p 18

Naisbitt J (1982) Megatrends: ten new directions transforming our lives. A Warner Communications Company, New York

Statistics and Census Service of the Government of Macao Special Administration Region (2018). Demographic statistics. https://www.dsec.gov.mo/Statistic.aspx?NodeGuid=7bb8808e-8fd3-4d6b-904a-34fe4b302883. Accessed 15 Oct 2018

UNESCO Office Bangkok and Regional Bureau for Education in Asia and the Pacific (2007) The UNESCO ICT in education programme. https://unesdoc.unesco.org/ark:/48223/pf0000231907.%20Accessed%2011%20Dec%202018. Accessed 10 Dec 2018

Zurkowski PG (1974) The information service environment relationships and priorities. Related paper no. 5. https://files.eric.ed.gov/fulltext/ED100391.pdf. Accessed 10 Nov 2018

Chapter 2
Information Search Strategies

Abstract This chapter introduces some commonly-used search strategies that can help improve your efficiency when finding useful information. These search strategies are applicable in all search tools and databases, with a few variations from one database to another. It is recommended that you read the "Help" section in each database before searching for the first time in a new database.

2.1 Boolean Searching

Boolean operators (named after mathematician George Boole) are AND, OR, and NOT. Boolean operators can be used to connect and define the relationship between search terms, and by doing so, narrow or broaden the search results.

AND: All your search terms will present in the retrieved results. Use this to narrow your results. For example, "business AND advertising" will find articles that contain both terms.

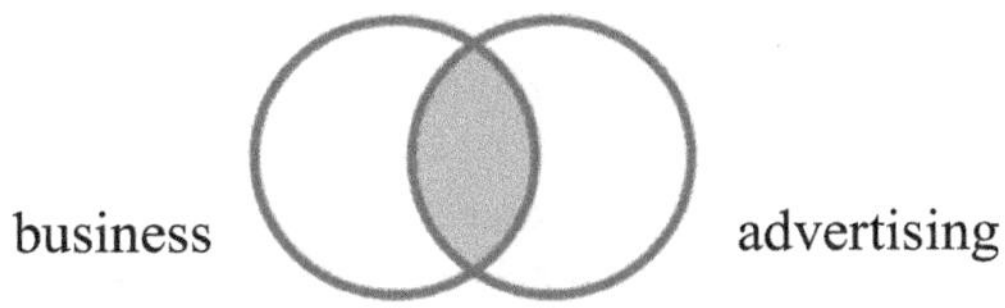

OR: At least one of your search terms will present in the retrieved results. Use as a way to broaden your search by connecting two or more synonyms. For example, "college OR university" finds results that contain either college or university, or both.

B. T. H. Leung et al., *Transferring Information Literacy Practices*,
https://doi.org/10.1007/978-981-13-7743-3_2

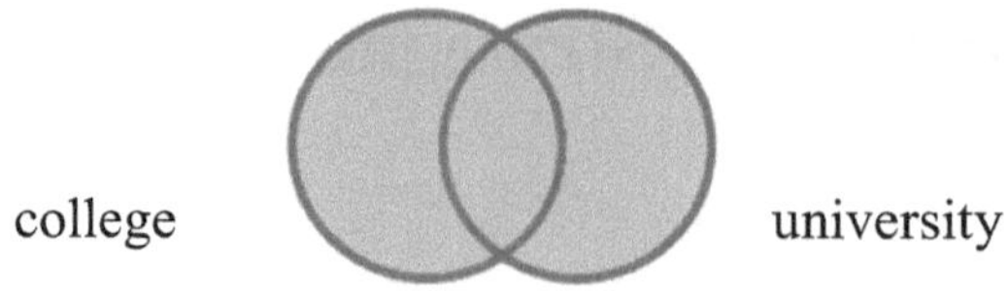

NOT: Excludes specific terms so that they do not present in the retrieved results. For example, "business NOT advertising" finds results that contain business but not advertising.

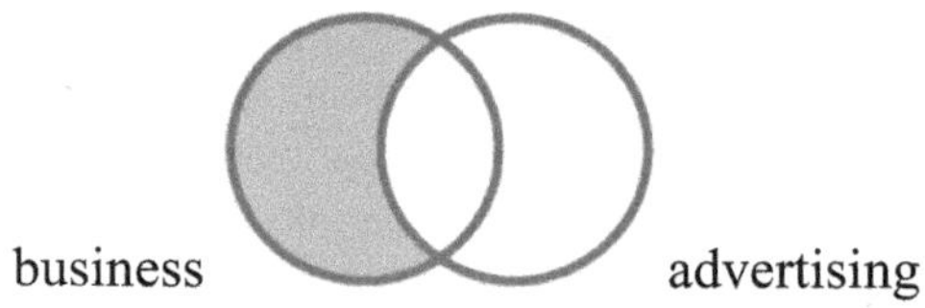

2.2 The Wildcard and Truncation Symbols

Wildcard and truncation symbols can be used to search words with unknown characters, multiple spellings or various endings. Neither the wildcard nor the truncation symbol can be used as the first character in a search term.

The most common wildcard/truncation symbols are the question mark (?), the pound or hash sign (#), and the asterisk (*). The question mark (?) matches one single letter. The pound or hash sign (#) matches zero or one letter. The asterisk (*) matches zero to multiple letters at the end of a word.

Using the ? wildcard: Enter your search terms and replace an unknown character with a ?. For example, ne?t will retrieve neat, nest, next, etc.

Using the # wildcard: Enter your search terms and place # where an alternate spelling might contain an extra character. For example, **colo#r** will retrieve color or colour.

Using the asterisk (*) truncation: Enter the root of a search term and replace the ending with an *. For example, **comput*** will retrieve **computer**, computing, computation, etc.

2.3 Proximity Search

Proximity search can be used to search for two or more words based on how closely they appear in the results.

The proximity operators are composed of a letter (**N** or **W**) and a **number** (to specify the number of words).

Near Operator (Nx)—finds words within x number of words from each other, regardless of the order in which they occur. For example, English **N5** learner will find "English learner", "learner of English", but not "learner of American English".

Within Operator (Wx)—finds words within x number of words from each other, in the order they are entered in the search. For example, English W8 learner will find "English learner", "English or French learner", but not "learner of English".

2.4 Grouping Terms Together Using Parentheses

When you use more than one Boolean Operator in your search, you could use parentheses to group search terms together and make them searched in the sequence you intend. Results differ accordingly.

The following example explains well the difference parentheses make:

For the same search terms and Boolean Operators:

loyalty AND consumer OR customer **versus** loyalty AND (consumer OR customer):

(1) If you do not use parentheses, as in loyalty AND consumer OR customer, terms with AND and NOT have priority over terms with OR, and therefore, loyalty and consumer will be searched first. In the final result set, loyalty and consumer either always appear together, or not at all, while customer may be the only term present.
(2) If you use parentheses, as in loyalty AND (consumer OR customer), elements that are enclosed in parentheses are executed first. That is to say, consumer OR customer will be searched first. In the final result set, consumer and customer may or may not be present, but loyalty will appear in every search result.

2.5 Use of Multiple Search Methods

Now let's try to use the search methods mentioned above in a search example. For the topic "brand loyalty and advertising", we may come up with a search string like the following:

(brand loyalty OR brand attachment) AND adverti*

By using a synonym of brand loyalty, we broaden our search to resources that deal with consumers' affection to a brand, which leads to loyalty as shown in buying choices. Note that the synonyms are enclosed with parentheses, meaning they are searched first. The Boolean Operator "AND" ensures that resulting records have to do with advertising. The truncation search enables us to find related words of advertising, such as advertisement, advertisements, etc.

2.6 Advanced Search Tips

Try using Advanced Search Operators, or field limiters, to search for a word or phrase in a specific part of the document (for example title or abstract) or within a certain website. To do this, place a field limiter before your search term followed by a colon.

Chapter 3
Resource Discovery Tools and Multi-disciplinary Databases

Abstract This chapter introduces the two most commonly used tools for academic resource retrieval, resource discovery services and multidisciplinary databases. You can use it as the first entry point in your research to find trusted and relevant resources.

3.1 Resource Discovery Tools

Resource discovery tools, sometimes called web scale discovery services, provide a one-stop search gateway for library users to easily find resources they need in their library's subscribed databases. By pre-harvesting and centrally indexing content sourced across multiple silos, web scale discovery services enable library users to simultaneously search across both physical and electronic resources available in the library, including physical holdings, such as books and DVDs; local electronic content, such as digital image collections and institutional repository materials; and remotely hosted content purchased or licensed by the library, such as e-books and publisher or aggregator content for thousands of full-text and abstracting and indexing sources.

Major web scale discovery services on the market include OCLC WorldCat Local, Serials Solutions Summon, EBSCO Discovery Service, Innovative Interfaces Encore Synergy, and Ex Libris Primo Central.

Library of University of Macau uses EBSCO Discovery Service, which allows library users to simultaneously search the print collection and various electronic databases for the information they need (Fig. 3.1).

B. T. H. Leung et al., *Transferring Information Literacy Practices*,
https://doi.org/10.1007/978-981-13-7743-3_3

Fig. 3.1 Discovery search of UM library, 2018 (http://library.umac.mo/)

3.1.1 Search in EBSCO Discovery Service

3.1.1.1 Basic Search

Simply enter your search terms in the search box. **Keyword** is the default search field. You may also use the drop-down menu beside the search box to conduct a **Title** search or an **Author** search (Fig. 3.2).

3.1.1.2 Advanced Search

Click the Advanced Search link below the basic search box. Enter your search terms in the search boxes on the Advanced Search screen, and choose a search field from the optional **Select a Field** drop-down list for each search box. Then select a

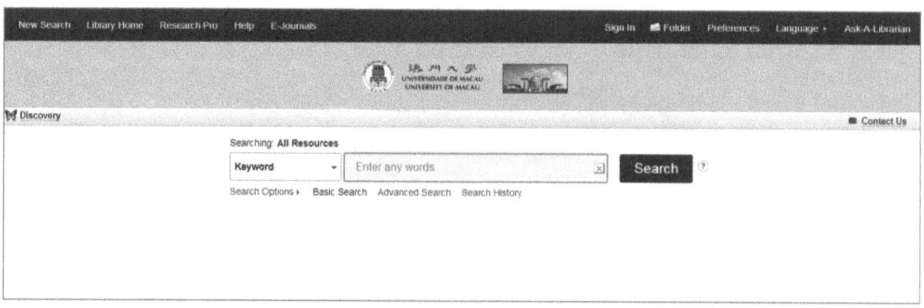

Fig. 3.2 Discovery search main Page, 2018 (http://eds.b.ebscohost.com/eds/search/basic)

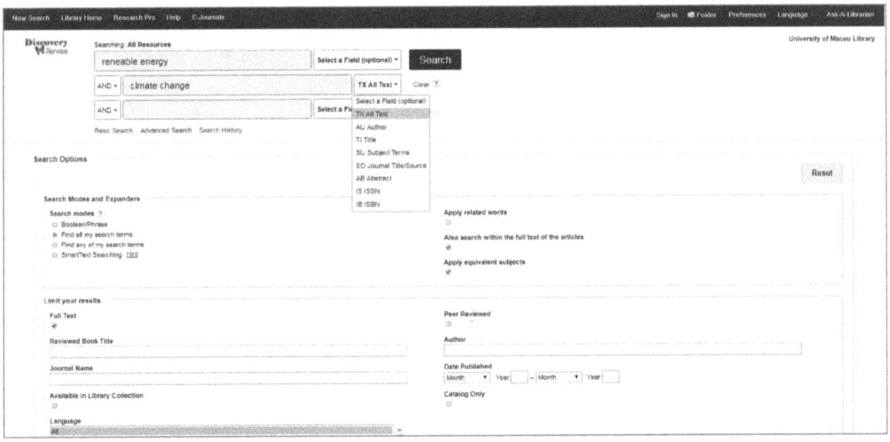

Fig. 3.3 Advance search of discovery search, 2018 (http://eds.b.ebscohost.com/eds/search/advanced)

Boolean operator (AND, OR, NOT) to combine your search terms. For additional rows, click the (+) link. To delete a row, click the (−) link (Fig. 3.3).

You can also use the search options below the search box to predefine your search results by:

- **Search modes**—such as "Find all of my search terms," or "SmartText Searching," or use search options that expand your search such as "Apply related words."
- **Limit your results**—such as Full Text or Publication type.
- **Special Limiters**—Apply limiters specific to a database. If you select a special limiter, it is applied only to the database under which it appears.

3.1.2 Search Results Page

The results page has 3 columns. The left column displays refinement tools to refine retrieved results. The middle column displays the search results. The right column lists additional information related to the search, such as images, blogs, widgets, and Web news (Fig. 3.4).

- Use the options in the left column to limit results to full text, peer reviewed, etc. You can also narrow results by source type, subject, journal, author, and more.
- Place your mouse over the Preview icon to view the Abstract of an article. The article title link will take you to the citation information and/or the full text in individual databases.

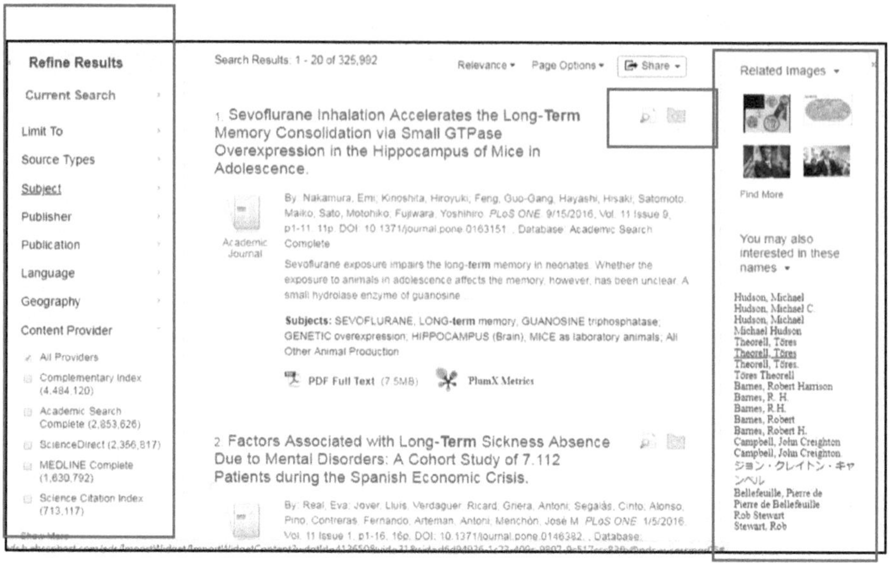

Fig. 3.4 Search results page of discovery search, 2018 (http://eds.b.ebscohost.com/eds/results)

Fig. 3.5 "My Folder" of discovery search, 2018 (http://eds.b.ebscohost.com/eds/detail)

- Click the **Folder** icon to the right of the article title to save an article temporarily or to your EBSCO folder. You can then email, print, or **export citations** using the folder screen (Fig. 3.5).

3.1.3 Cite

EBSCO Discovery Service provides pre-formatted citations in a few commonly used styles for users to copy and download.

Click on the title of a record on the result list to go to the article page. Then click "Cite" link on the right column. You can either copy or paste the citation of your chosen style into a document, or you may export the citations to reference management software by clicking the "Export" link on the right (Figs. 3.6 and 3.7).

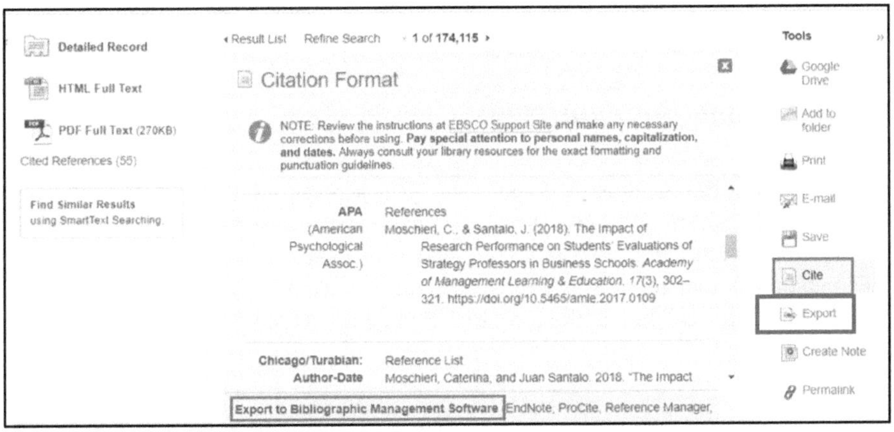

Fig. 3.6 "Citation Format" of discovery search, 2018 (http://eds.b.ebscohost.com/eds/detail)

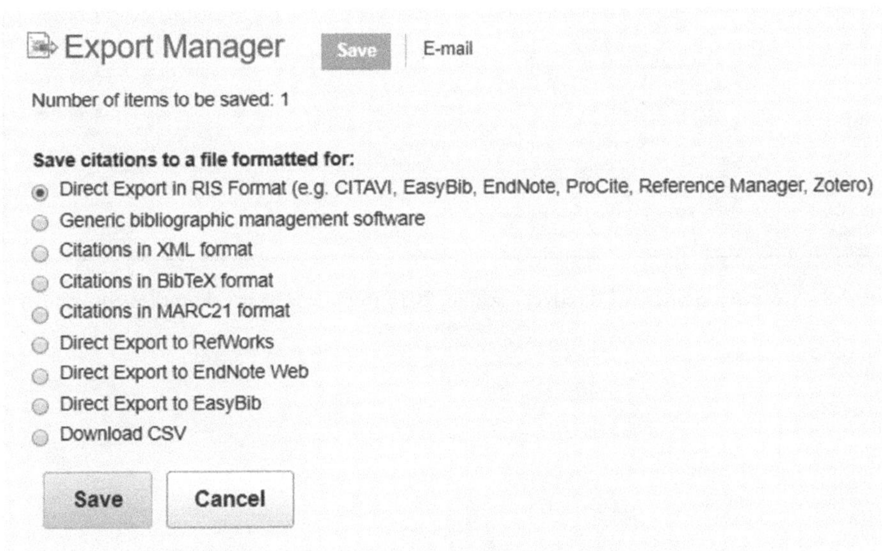

Fig. 3.7 "Export manager" of discovery search, 2018 (http://eds.b.ebscohost.com/eds/detail)

3.1.4 Research Starters

When a user conducts a search in EDS, a Research Starter placard (outlined below in red) may appear at the top of the Result List. For those topics identified as most popular, Research Starters will retrieve relevant articles that link the user to related information and detailed bibliographies.

Research Starters content is organized from a variety of high quality sources, both proprietary and encyclopedic, including Salem Press, Encyclopædia Britannica, and others. Simply click the article **title** or the **More** button to read about the topic or to find related articles and images (Fig. 3.8).

3.1.5 Personal Account

A personal My EBSCOhost account gives you a personal area (folder) to collect and store information across sessions. You can save search results, persistent links to searches, search alerts, journal alerts, and web pages. All the items you save to your personal folder remain in your folder until you remove them.

Click the "Sign in" link at the top of EDS page to create your personal account in EDS (Fig. 3.9).

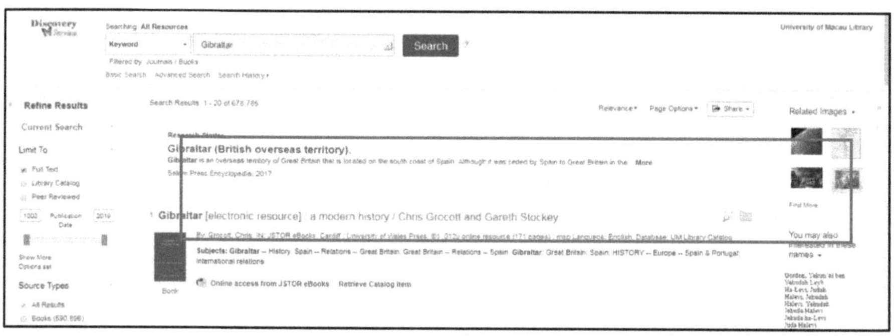

Fig. 3.8 "Research Starter" of discovery search, 2018 (http://eds.b.ebscohost.com/eds/results)

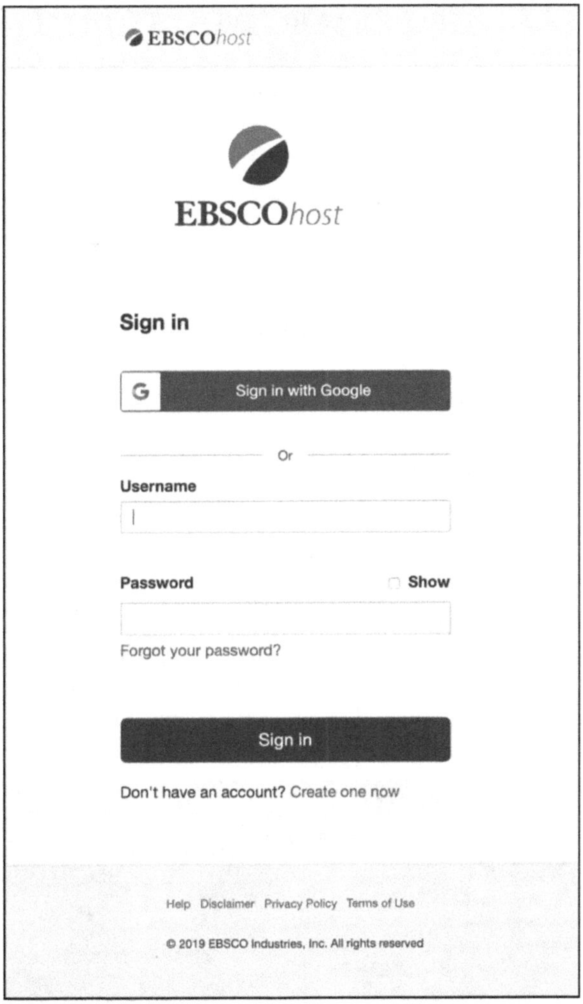

Fig. 3.9 Personal login to discovery search, 2018 (https://auth.ebsco.zone/api/oidcprovider/)

3.2 Multi-disciplinary Databases

Multidisciplinary databases provide many reliable full-texts and/or abstracts of academic journal articles, newspaper/magazine articles, books, conference proceedings, reports, etc. from different publishers, covering a wide range of subjects in the humanities, social sciences, sciences, technology, and medicine.

University of Macau subscribes to a number of multidisciplinary databases, such as ProQuest Central, JSTOR, Scopus, etc. We will use ProQuest Central as our example of how to search in multidisciplinary databases. These search methods can be applied to other multidisciplinary databases, as well.

3.2.1 *Introduction to ProQuest Central*

ProQuest Central is the largest single periodical resource available, bringing together complete databases across all major subject areas, including Business, Health and Medical, Language and Literature, Social Sciences, Education, Science and Technology, as well as core titles in the Performing and Visual Arts, History, Religion, Philosophy, and thousands of full-text newspapers from around the world.

3.2.2 *Search on ProQuest Central*

3.2.2.1 Basic Search

Simply enter search words and click Search (Fig. 3.10).

3.2.2.2 Advanced Search

Enter your search words in the search boxes, and select a search field for each of them. Then select Boolean Operators to connect the search terms (Fig. 3.11).

You can limit your search to full text, scholarly journals, peer reviewed, date range, source type, document type, etc. (Fig. 3.12).

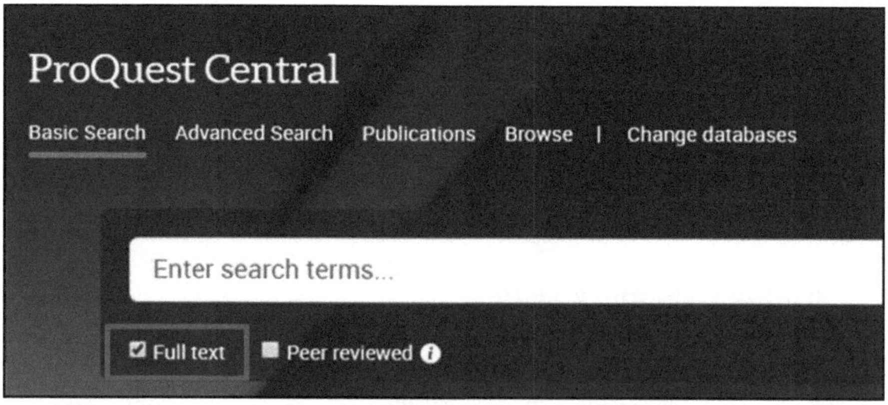

Fig. 3.10 Main page of ProQuest central (https://search.proquest.com/central)

Fig. 3.11 Tab linking to ProQuest central advanced search (https://search.proquest.com/central)

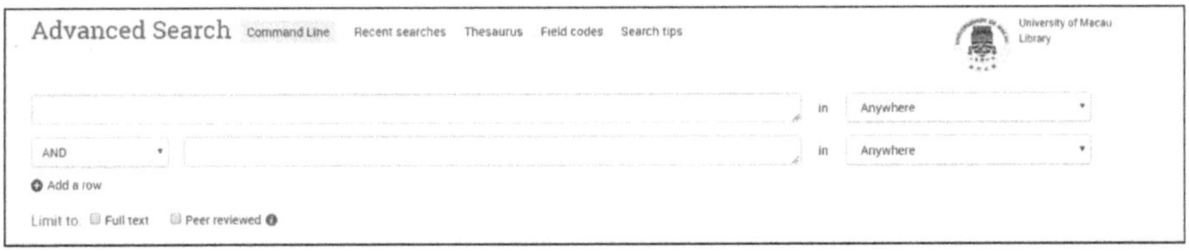

Fig. 3.12 ProQuest central advanced search main page (https://search.proquest.com/central/advanced)

3.2.2.3 Thesaurus

A thesaurus is an alphabetical listing of all the subject terms in a single database. It can be used to classify and organize information for that database. The thesaurus shows relationships between terms such as synonymous or related terms, and hierarchical arrangements such as broader terms, or narrower terms. Many subjects also have associated scope notes.

Click the "Thesaurus" link located on the top line of the Advanced Search page. Select one or more thesaurus terms, and add them to your search (Fig. 3.13).

Beside each thesaurus term, there is an "Explode" checkbox. As database documents usually are indexed to the most specific term possible, if you choose a broad index term, you may not retrieve all useful documents. Checking the "Explode" box asks to search a subject term and all its associated narrower terms. This way, you can retrieve all potentially useful documents using a broad topic (Fig. 3.14).

3.2.3 Search Results

On the search result page, use the narrowing filters on the left to refine your search results. Available filters include: subject, date, company/organization, etc.

You can cite, email, print, or save the results using the links available at the top right of the page, immediately above your results.

You can also select several records at the same time before you cite, email, print, or save them (Fig. 3.15).

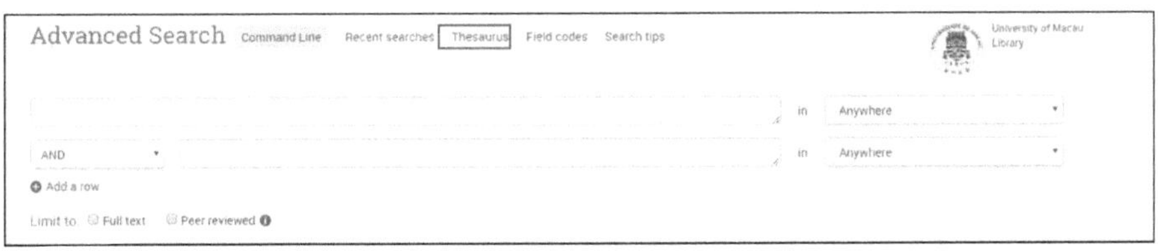

Fig. 3.13 Tab linking to thesaurus of ProQuest central databases (https://search.proquest.com/central/advanced)

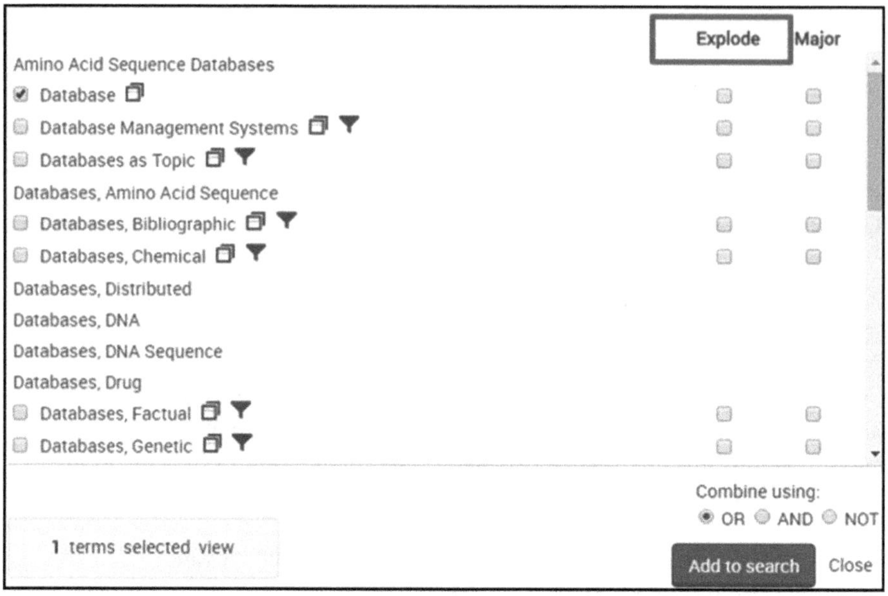

Fig. 3.14 "Explode" Checkbox of ProQuest central (https://search.proquest.com/central/advanced)

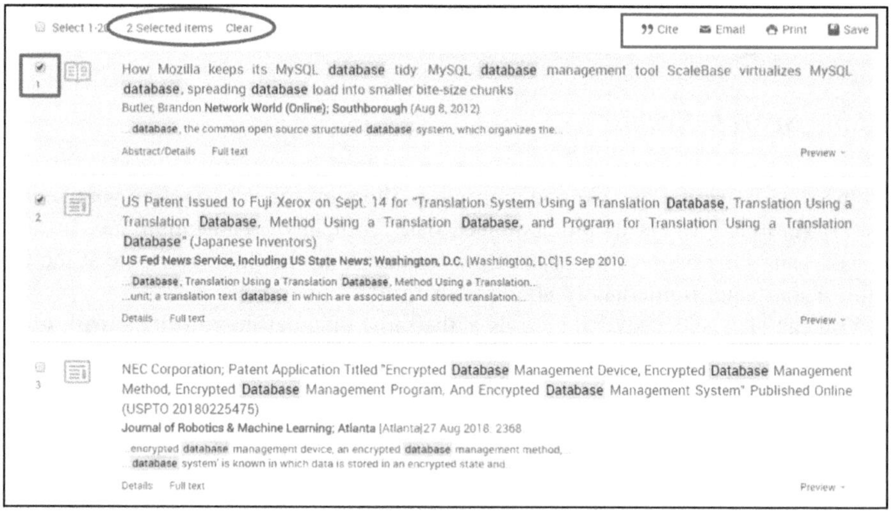

Fig. 3.15 Search result page of ProQuest central (https://search.proquest.com/central/results)

3.2.4 *Cite*

To create a formatted citation in your preferred citation style, select the checkbox in front of a record, and click the "Cite" link at the top right of the page. You can then email, print, or download the citations. You may also wish to copy and paste the citations into a Word or other document (Fig. 3.16).

3.2.5 *Save: Export/Save*

With one or more documents selected in your results list, click options on the Save menu beneath the Export/Save heading (Fig. 3.17).

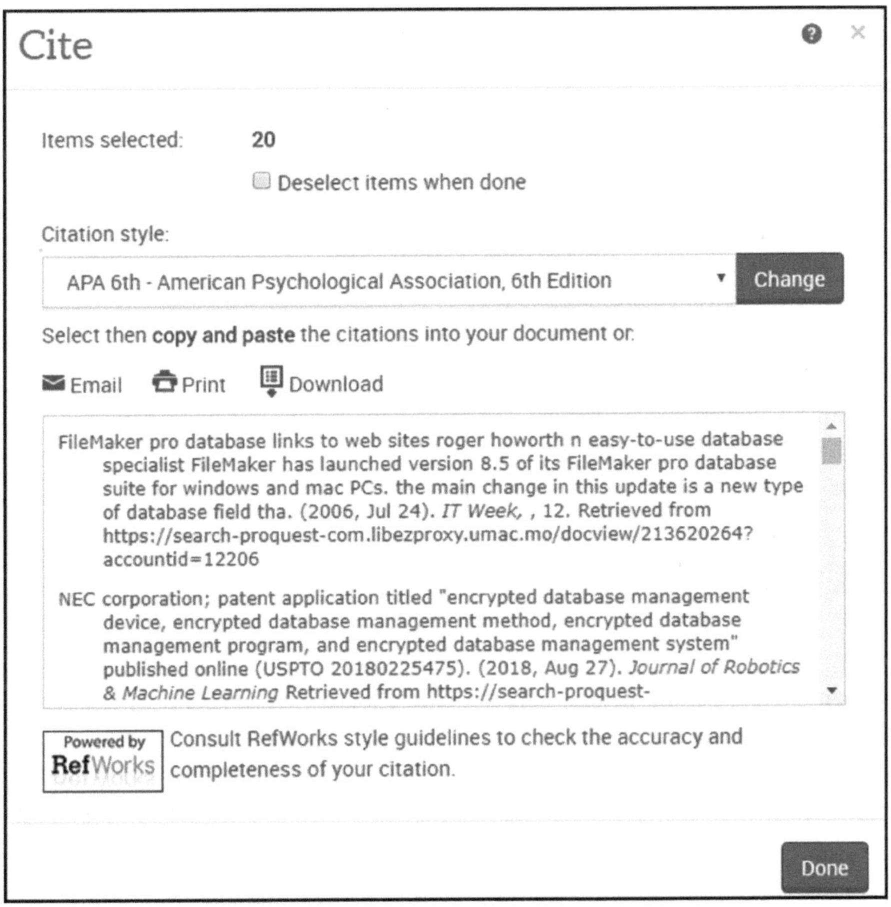

Fig. 3.16 Citation generated by ProQuest central (https://search.proquest.com/central/results)

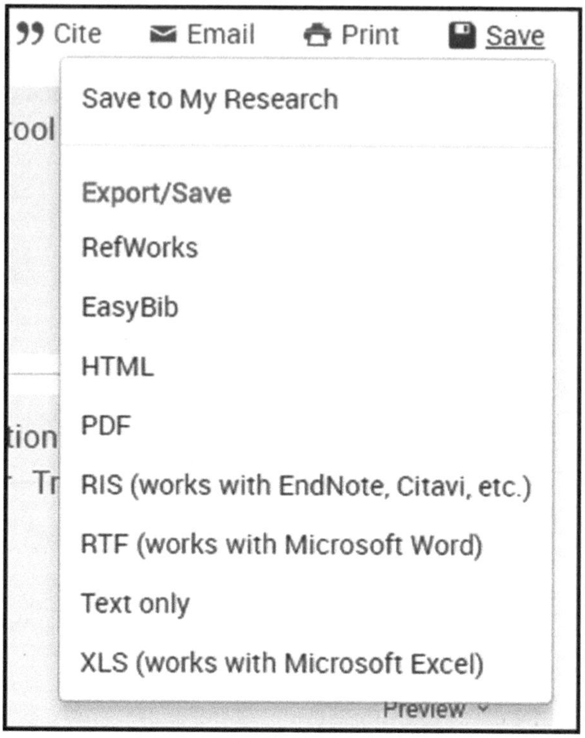

Fig. 3.17 Export/save citation of ProQuest central (https://search.proquest.com/central/results)

- Export document citations to a:
  - citation management tool, such as RefWorks
  - formatted text file, such as RIS
  - reporting tool, such as Excel
- Or, save document information to file formats such as PDF or Text only.

3.2.6 My Research Account

Creating a My Research account enables you to save, manage, and organize the content and supporting materials you find in ProQuest. Things you can do in My Research include:

- Save documents and searches across several ProQuest sessions.
- Create folders to save and manage documents you find relevant to your research.
- Save and manage search alerts, publication alerts, and RSS feeds.

Chapter 4
Information Literacy General Resources, Tools and How to Access Them

Abstract This chapter introduces the print and electronic general resources and tools for each discipline in the University of Macau Library and how to access and use them.

4.1 Encyclopedias and Dictionaries

You have probably already used encyclopedias and dictionaries at some point in your schooling career.

Dictionaries simply provide brief definitions of words, terms and acronyms. Through the UM Library, you can access a number of the most commonly-used electronic dictionaries.

It is relatively simple to access UM Library subscribed Encyclopedias and Dictionaries from the Library's homepage. Follow the path given in Figs. 4.1 and 4.2.

4.2 Highlighted Dictionary

4.2.1 Oxford English Dictionary

The Oxford English Dictionary (OED) is widely-regarded as the accepted authority on the English language. It is an unsurpassed guide to the meaning, history, and pronunciation of 600,000 words—past and present—from across the English-speaking world.

B. T. H. Leung et al., *Transferring Information Literacy Practices*,
https://doi.org/10.1007/978-981-13-7743-3_4

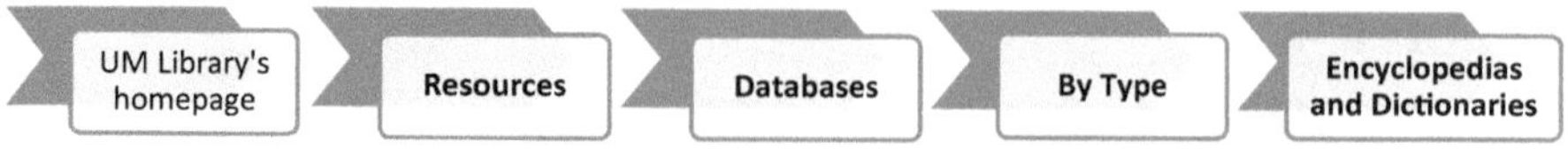

Fig. 4.1 Link path to go to UM library subscribed encyclopedias and dictionaries

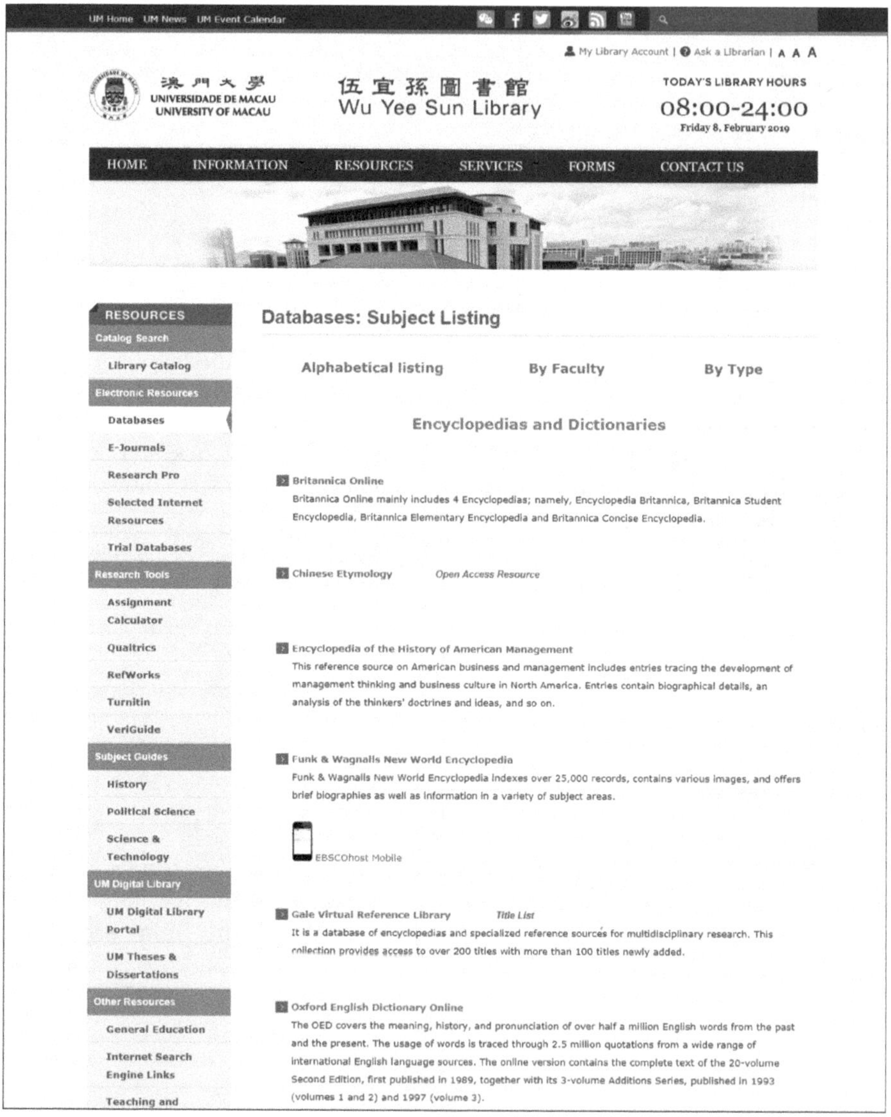

Fig. 4.2 UM library subscribed encyclopedias and dictionaries (https://library.umac.mo/html/databases/e_databases_id_res.asp?getsuid=18)

Fig. 4.3 Main page of "Oxford English Dictionary" (www.oed.com)

As a historical dictionary, the OED is very different from other dictionaries of current English, in which the focus is on present-day meanings. You'll still find present-day meanings in the OED, but you'll also find the history of individual words. You'll also find histories of the English language traced through 3 million quotations, from classic literature and specialist periodicals to film scripts and even cookery books (Fig. 4.3).

Encyclopedias are very useful for learning basic background information about a topic. They help especially when you are dealing with a completely unfamiliar or complex topic. Many provide short bibliographies in their entries, which then lead you to key readings to help you learn more about a particular topic. We will look at this type of resource in detail in the discipline-specific units within this chapter, but first, let's note some of the key points of those highlighted above.

4.3 Highlighted Encyclopedias

4.3.1 Britannica® Academic

Britannica® Academic delivers fast, easy access to high-quality information. You may already be familiar with Encyclopedia Britannica, as it has been in use by students and scholars for a long time. Add to that Merriam-Webster's Collegiate Dictionary, a variety of magazines and periodicals, and many other research tools and you have a variety of reliable sources to consult when conducting research—all from one resource (Fig. 4.4).

4.3.2 The Oxford Encyclopedia of the Modern World

This encyclopedia provides information about major world developments from 1750 to the present, giving close attention to social, economic, cultural, and political topics. It contains articles on world events, countries, organizations, regions, ethnic groups, and themes (Fig. 4.5).

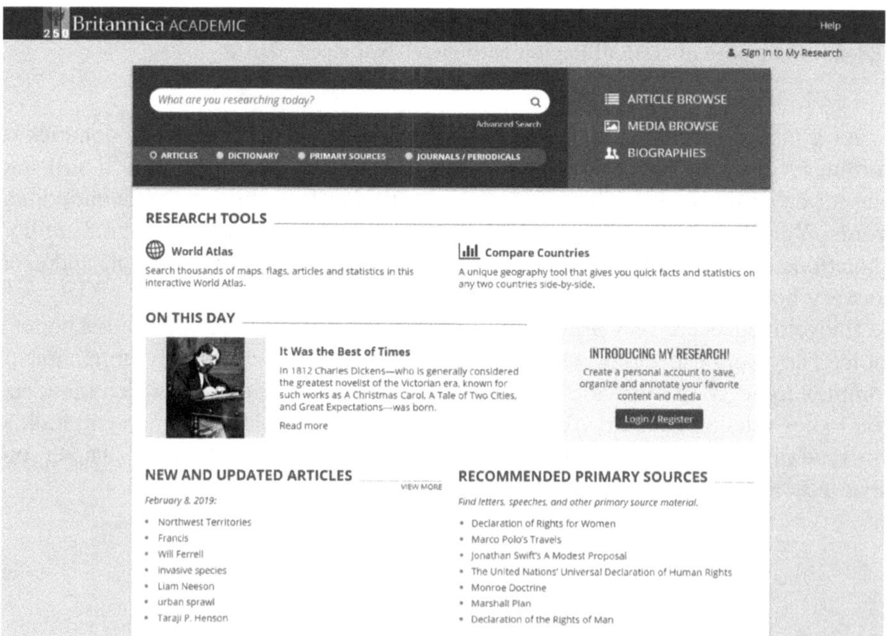

Fig. 4.4 Main page of "Britannica® Academic" (https://academic.eb.com/levels/collegiate)

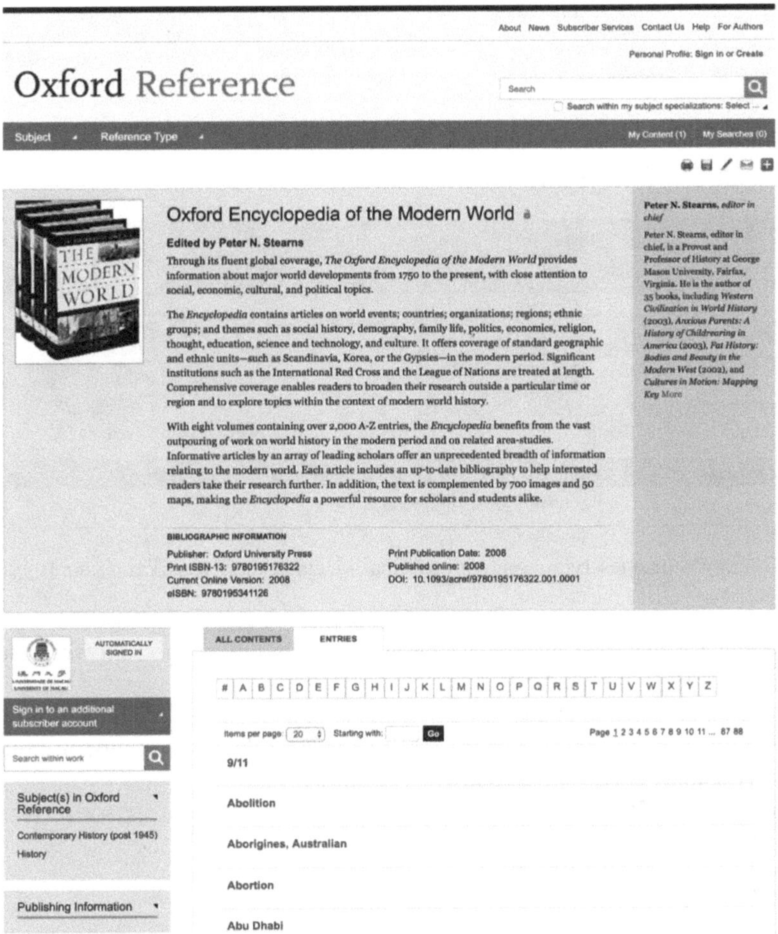

Fig. 4.5 Main page of "Oxford Reference" (www.oxfordreference.com)

4.4 Course Reserves

Sometimes professors work with the library to make sure you have access to specialized materials for particular courses. Please note that, because these are for all students in a course, you may only use them while in the library (LIB USE ONLY). Course reserve services gives you access to class materials, which may take the form of books, photocopied articles, textbooks, class notes, old tests, or even video or sound recordings.

UM Library maintains a collection of reserved materials for courses at the Ground Floor Zone C1 Circulation Counter.

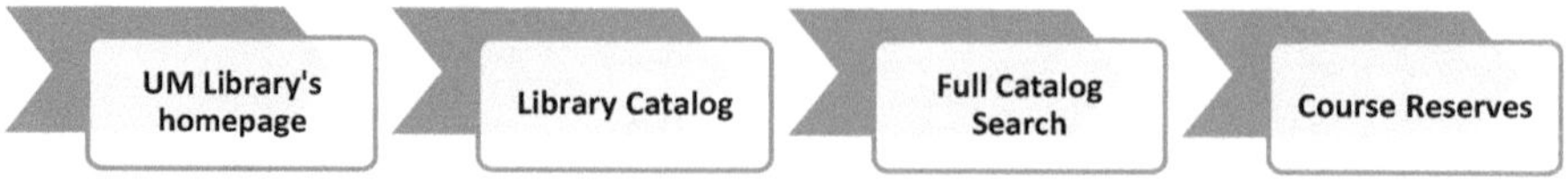

Fig. 4.6 Link path to go to UM course reserves catalog (by the author)

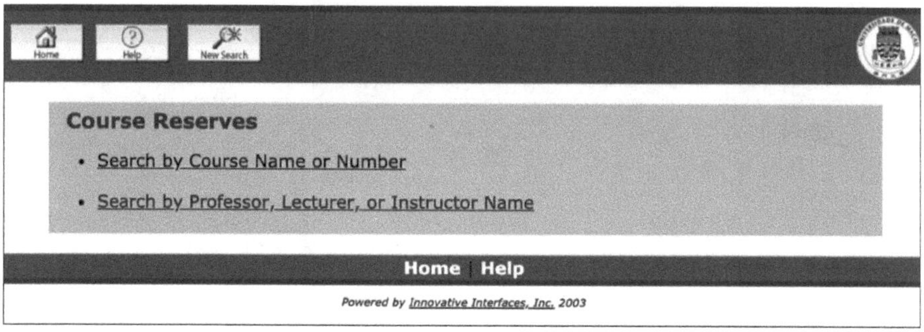

Fig. 4.7 UM library course reserves catalog (http://umaclib3.umac.mo/screens/course.html)

Please search for reserved materials in UM Library's homepage following the steps are given in Figs. 4.6 and 4.7.

There are two ways of searching Course Reserves: by course name/number or by professor/lecture/instructor name. Decide which you wish to use and type in your search term. A sample result page follows (Fig. 4.8).

Click on the title of a record to view details (Fig. 4.9).

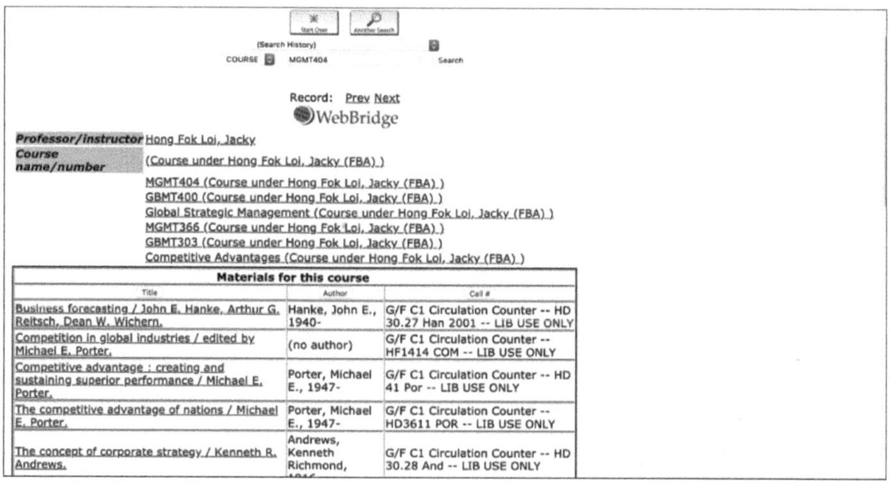

Fig. 4.8 Course reserves search result page (http://umaclib3.umac.mo/search/r?SEARCH=MGMT404&submit=Submit)

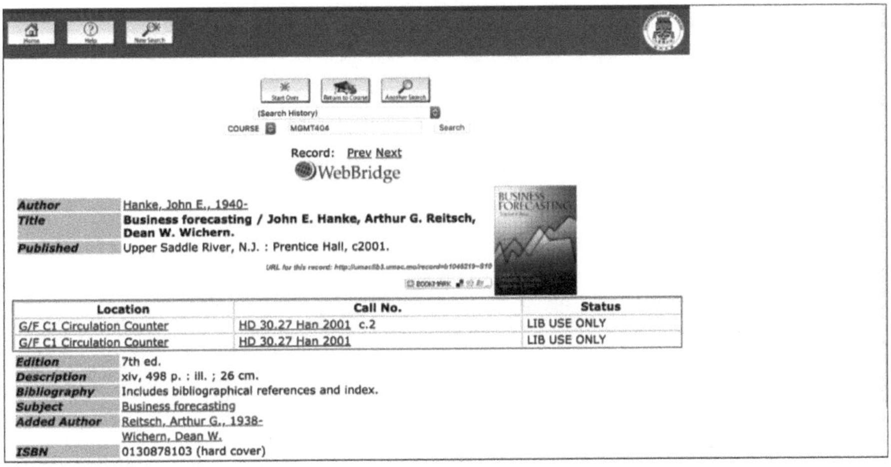

Fig. 4.9 One of the materials detailed information for a course (http://umaclib3.umac.mo/search~S10)

4.5 Finding Aid

4.5.1 Discovery Search

A discovery service is an online library searching tool that provides an all-in-one interface for finding both local library items and online subscription and open access resources. Refer to the previous chapter for detailed introduction to UM Library's discovery service.

4.5.2 Library Catalog

You can access the library catalog directly using the UM library's website.

The Library Catalog can be used to locate a record of virtually any item in the library's holdings. This record will then tell you where to find the item in the library (or where you can access it on-line) and can be used to point you to similar items. You may want to begin by seeing the types of resources available. Macau has a rich history, and some of the special collections are unique and rare (Fig. 4.10).

The following are the results of a search by title for "Matteo Ricci". UM Library has 8 records with "Matteo Ricci" in their titles. If you want additional information regarding each individual record–for example, the date it was published, and if there are any notes or additional information describing the item, simply click on its title (Fig. 4.11).

Fig. 4.10 Library catalog search of "Matteo Ricci" by title (http://library.umac.mo/)

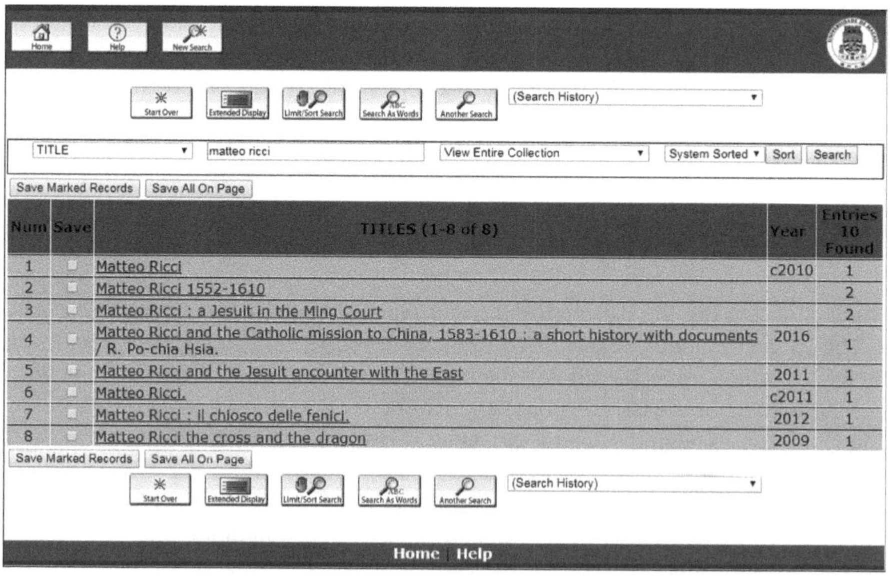

Fig. 4.11 Search result of "Matteo Ricci" by title on UM library catalog (http://umaclib3.umac.mo/search/?searchtype=t&searcharg=Matteo+Ricci&submit=)

Fig. 4.12 Detailed information on one search result of "Matteo Ricci" by title on UM library catalog (http://umaclib3.umac.mo/search ~ S10)

You will then see a page with detailed information to find the item in the library. You only need three pieces of information to quickly locate the material: Library Location, Call Number, and Status (Fig. 4.12).

Location: The Library Location will inform you which section of the library the material is in. We can see that the version of Matteo Ricci in our example is located on the 2nd floor Zone A3.

Call Number: The Call Number will allow you to pinpoint the book's location. Materials use the Library of Congress Classification System.

Status: Indicates if the material is checked in (therefore available to be checked out), or otherwise missing. If a title is checked out, you can still enter the title's record and request a hold–you will be notified where you are in line and when the book is due back.

If a title is an electronic resource, you could click into the record (see Fig. 4.13). From there, click on the Web Link to be directed to the database containing the material. Note that you will need your UM PASS Login and Password.

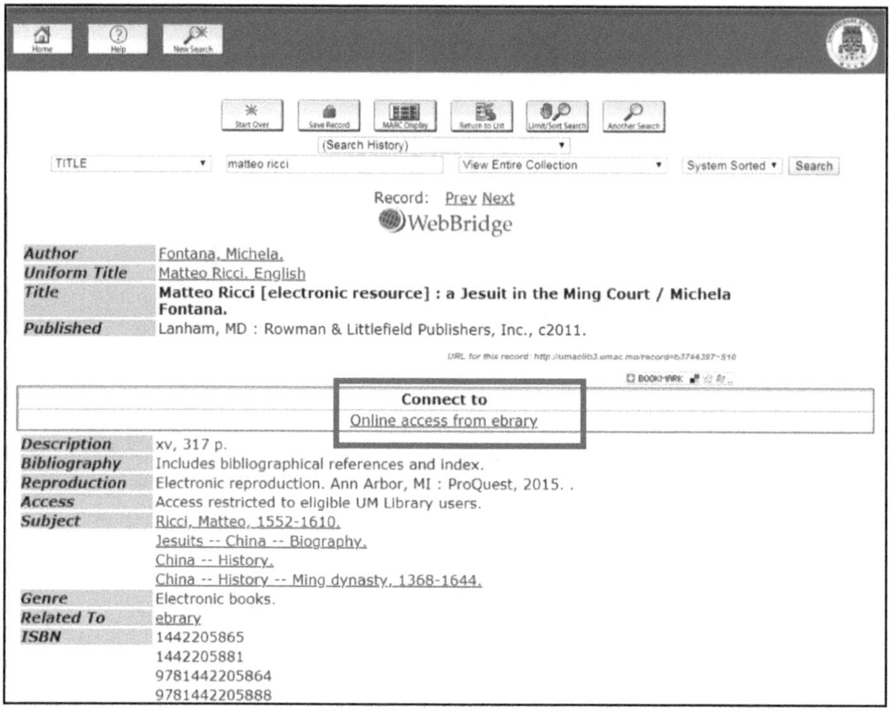

Fig. 4.13 Detailed information on another search result of "Matteo Ricci" by title on UM library catalog (http://umaclib3.umac.mo/search ~ S10)

4.5.3 E-journal Search

Serious scholars appreciate UM Library's access to full text e-journals. Electronic information repositories typically include electronic journals, conference proceedings, and reports. This wealth of scholarly information to support your research is easily accessed from the Library's homepage. If you already know the name of the e-journal you wish to use, you can search for it by title or ISSN using the E-journal search tab on UM library's homepage (Fig. 4.14).

At the E-journal search main page, you can further search by journal title, browse an alphabetical listing of individual journal titles, and/or browse journal collections arranged by publisher (Fig. 4.15).

In the example below, we selected the "Language and Linguistics" subcategory under the subject area of "Arts and Humanities" . There are 1723 individual e-journal titles catalogued under these headings (Fig. 4.16).

To find materials relevant to your research, you will often need to consult a variety of different e-journals, thus covering a range of academic subject areas relevant to.

Fig. 4.14 E-journal search of UM library (http://library.umac.mo/)

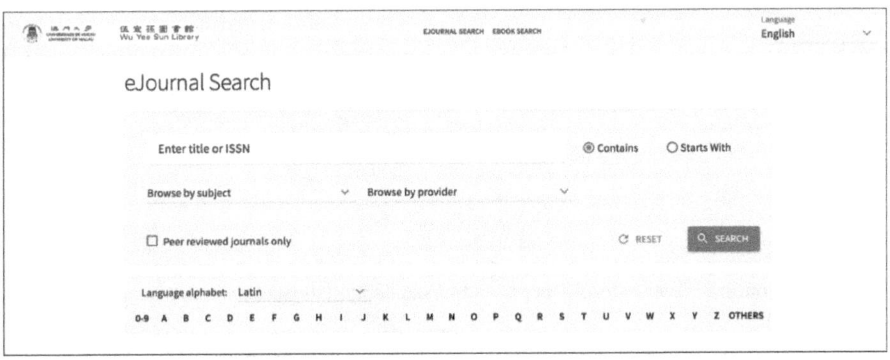

Fig. 4.15 E-journal search main page (http://sfx-853uom.hosted.exlibrisgroup.com/853uom/journalsearch)

4.5.4 Multidisciplinary Databases

Multidisciplinary databases cover a wide range of academic subjects including the arts, health care, business, literature, law, sciences, and more from journals, newspapers, magazines, ebooks, and reports.

Some multidisciplinary databases and providers are:

Fig. 4.16 E-journal search result page (http://sfx-853uom.hosted.exlibrisgroup.com/853uom/journalsearch)

4.5.4.1 Academic OneFile

Academic OneFile provides peer-reviewed, full text articles from journals and reference sources. Subjects and disciplines covered include biology, chemistry, criminal justice, economics, environmental science, history, marketing, political science, and psychology.

4.5.4.2 Academic Search Complete

Academic Search Complete features thousands of full-text journals. This scholarly collection offers unmatched coverage spanning a broad range of academic study/ Subjects include: anthropology, astronomy, biology, chemistry, civil engineering, engineering, ethnic and multicultural studies, geology, law, materials science, mathematics, music, pharmaceutical sciences, physics, psychology, religion and theology, veterinary science, women's studies, zoology, and many other fields.

4.5.4.3 Jstor

JSTOR's (Journal Storage) archives include scholarship published in over one thousand of the highest-quality academic journals across the humanities, social sciences, and sciences.

4.5.4.4 ProQuest Central

ProQuest Central is a comprehensive multidisciplinary research database. It provides access to databases across all major subject areas, including business, health and medical, social sciences, arts and humanities, education, science and technology, and religion. The collection includes thousands of full-text scholarly journals, newspapers, magazines, dissertations, working papers, and market reports all together in one platform.

4.5.4.5 ScienceDirect

ScienceDirect provides full text online access to over 4500 Elsevier journals and ebooks. The Backfiles program offers the ability to search a historical archive of over 6.75 million articles. This set of journals is a key component of Healey Library's online scholarly journal collection.

4.5.4.6 Scopus

Scopus is a citation database of research literature. This database provides searching capability, linking to full-text sources, cited references, saved search and alerting feature.

4.5.4.7 Web of Science

Web of Science is a research platform that gives you access to objective content and powerful tools to search, track, measure and collaborate in the sciences, social sciences, arts, and humanities. This intelligent research platform provides access to the world's leading citation databases, including powerful cited reference searching, the Analyze Tool, and over up to 100 years of comprehensive backfile and citation data.

4.5.4.8 Wiley Online Library

Wiley Online Library allows online access to the full text of over 400 journals and more than 2,300 titles of ebooks, which covers a wide range of subjects such as business, management, psychology, humanities and social science, science and engineering etc.

For a detailed introduction to multidisciplinary databases, please refer to Chap. 3.

4.5.5 Google Scholar

Google Scholar is a Web search engine that specifically searches scholarly literature and academic resources. It searches the same kinds of scholarly books, articles, and documents as you do in the Library's catalog and databases. The scholarly, authoritative focus of Google Scholar distinguishes it from ordinary Google. We will look at Google Scholar in details in Chap. 7.

While searching with these search engines, apply search techniques like those presented in Chap. 2: Information Searching Strategies, to make your search more efficient.

4.6 Conference Proceedings

Conference papers present the latest research and advancements in a particular field. Therefore, conference papers and proceedings can be a great source of current research and leading information in a field. DeFelice describes how: "Usually, a scientific meeting, convention or conference covers a range of topics within a subject area. Attendees participate in seminars, discussion groups, lectures and/or poster sessions. The oral presentations at these meetings are called conference papers. The collective group of conference papers is called the conference proceedings. Other commonly used terms include symposia, colloquium, congress, discussion, institute, seminar, meeting, session, summer school or workshop." (DeFelice 1995).

Table 4.1 Common synonyms for conference proceedings

Congresses	Colloquium
Meetings	Workshop
Symposium	Transaction

Adapted from University of Waterloo Library (2018)

A conference proceeding is the published record of a conference, congress, symposium, or other meeting sponsored by a society or association, usually but not necessarily including abstracts or reports of papers presented by the participants. When the entire text of the papers presented is included, the result is called transactions.

Synonyms for Conference Proceedings (Table 4.1).

Use these alternate terms when searching for conference proceedings:

Abbreviations: cong., symp., congr., proc., etc.

Note: Not all conferences publish proceedings, and not all published proceedings are peer-reviewed. Also, not all journals that have the word "Proceedings" in their titles are conference proceedings.

4.6.1 Databases with Conference Proceedings

Conference papers are important research resources for some specific disciplines, especially in medicine, computer science, physics, biology, and engineering. The following list show subject specific databases that index conference proceedings.

4.6.1.1 ACM Digital Library: Association for Computing Machinery

Full text of every article ever published by ACM and bibliographic citations from major publishers in computing. After doing a search for ACM articles, you can expand your search to The ACM Guide to Computing Literature (Bibliographic citations from major publishers in computing).

4.6.1.2 ArXiv

Open access to e-prints in Physics, Mathematics, Computer Science, Quantitative Biology, Quantitative Finance and Statistics.

4.6.1.3 Bio Web of Conferences

BIO Web of Conferences is an open access venue for archiving conference proceedings in biology.

4.6.1.4 British Library. The Conference Collections

The British Library conference index contains the records of 400,000 conference proceedings held in stock, with 16,000 new records added each year.

4.6.1.5 EI Compendex

It is a bibliographic database on engineering research, containing over 9 million records and references over 5,000 international engineering sources including journal, conference, and trade publications.

4.6.1.6 EJP Web of Conferences

Open-access proceedings in pure and applied physics, including materials science, physical biology, physical chemistry, and complex systems.

4.6.1.7 Elsevier Procedia

Procedia are e-only conference proceedings published in dedicated open-access issues on ScienceDirect. There are a wide variety of subject series, including: Energy; Chemistry; Environmental Sciences; as well as conferences sponsored by various societies (IUTAM, IERE, AASRI, etc.).

4.6.1.8 ESAIM (European Series in Applied and Industrial Mathematics): Proceedings

ESAIM Proceedings includes colloquia, seminars, summer schools, etc., in all areas of applied mathematics.

4.6.1.9 IEEE Xplore

IEEE Xplore provides full-text access to IEEE transactions, journals, magazines and conference proceedings published since 1988 and all current IEEE standards.

4.6.1.10 IOP Conference Series: Materials Science and Engineering (MSE)

As an open-access title, MSE will make conference papers available to material scientists, physicists, chemists and engineers.

4.6.1.11 Inspec

This bibliographic database provides abstracts and indexing to the world's scientific and technical papers in physics, electrical engineering, electronics, communications, control engineering, computing, information technology, manufacturing, production and mechanical engineering.

4.6.1.12 Journal of Physics: Conference Series

An open-access journal with conference proceedings in each volume, from the year 2004.

4.6.1.13 Web of Conferences

Web of Conferences is a scientific conference portal that collects both open access and subscription based conference proceedings series and journals published by EDP Sciences.

4.7 Inter-library Loan and Document Delivery Services

Sometime you may need of books and journal articles not available at our UM library. Inter-Library Loan and Document Delivery Services helps you get them from other libraries. Logon to UM library Inter-Library Loan system (ILLiad) and send requests.

More information is available through UM library's homepage (Figs. 4.17, 4.18, 4.19 and 4.20).

4.7.1 Delivery Time

The average time required to obtain copies from another source is three days to two weeks. Time for book requests that must be sent to Hong Kong or overseas is usually three to four weeks, which may sometimes take considerably longer than this average (Guidelines for Interlibrary Loan/Document Delivery Service 2018).

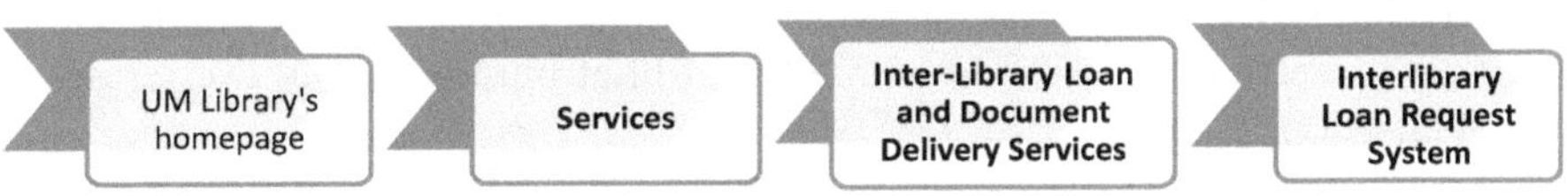

Fig. 4.17 Link path to go to UM library interlibrary loan request system (by the author)

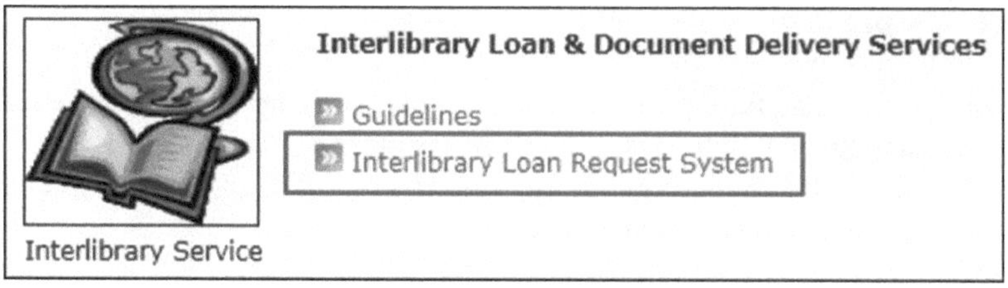

Fig. 4.18 Link to UM library interlibrary loan request system (http://library.umac.mo/html/services/reference/reference.html#ILL)

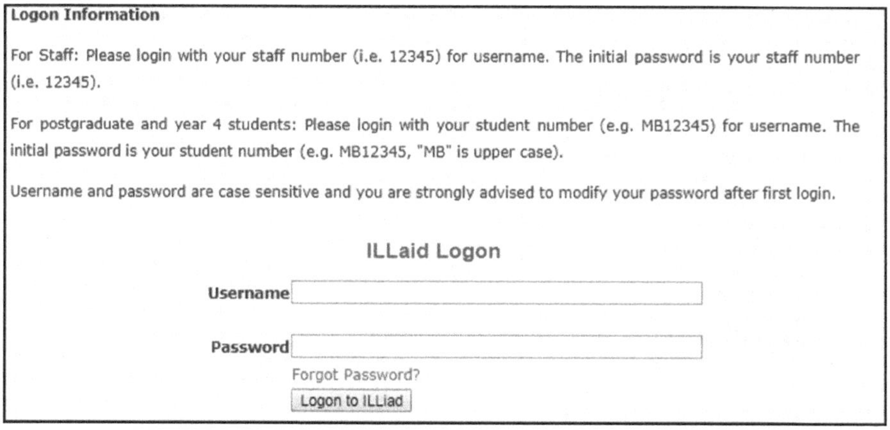

Fig. 4.19 UM library interlibrary loan request system logon page (http://library.umac.mo/html/services/inter_loan/ill_main.html)

4.8 Research Tools

Research tools enable researchers and modelers to construct theories and system models. They typically support capturing hypotheses, inferring mechanisms, and formulating experimental results within the same framework. Among the key features of such tools are convenient ways to represent several competing theories and the interactive nature of building and running the models using a rigorous scenario-based language. Professional software tools also let the researcher visualize complex interrelations between phenomena and provide quantifiable reporting capabilities.

UM Library has subscribed to/developed various research tools. The following parts of this section provide you with a list of brief introduction to every research tool (Fig. 4.21).

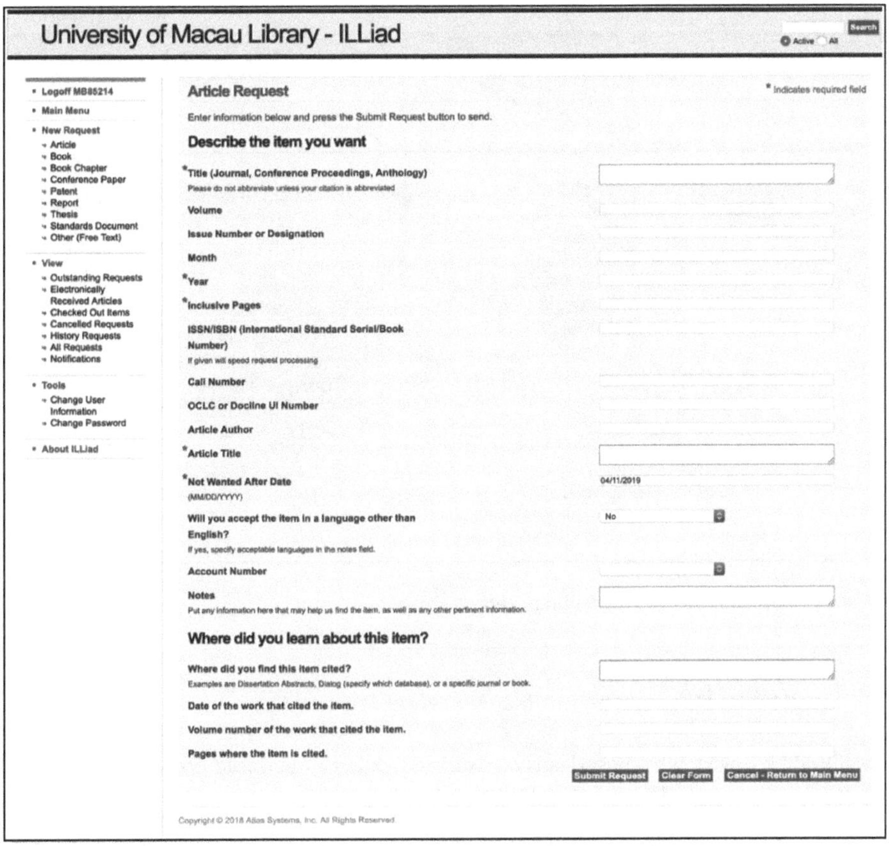

Fig. 4.20 Main page of UM library interlibrary loan request system (https://umac-mo.illiad.oclc.org/illiad/illiad.dll)

4.8.1 Assignment Calculator

Assignment Calculator is a Time Management Tool for Doing Research and Writing Your Paper. It can help you determine how much time you have to complete various aspects of your research and writing, given your starting date and due date. This Assignment Calculator also allocates online resources which can assist you in executing each step (Assignment Calculator 2018).

4.8.2 EndNote

EndNote is a tool that allows you to collect bibliographic references in a library, organize and manage those references, and ultimately put them in the body of a paper and in a reference list in a desired citation format.

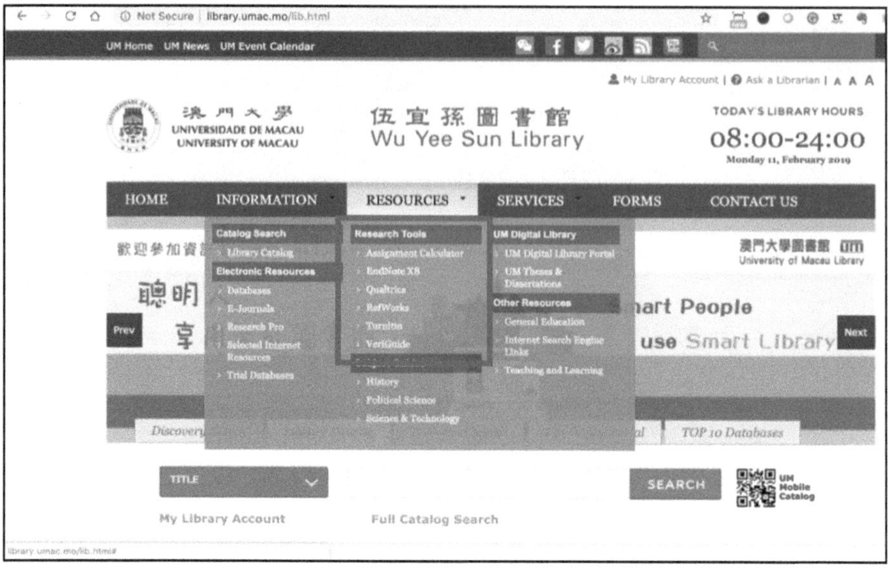

Fig. 4.21 Research tools of UM library (http://library.umac.mo/)

4.8.3 *Qualtrics*

UM-Qualtrics is a web-based survey service that is available for use by all UM faculty, staff and students. UM-Qualtrics is useful to:

- Assist faculty, staff, and students with creating online surveys and collecting data for research projects or assignments.
- Assess user satisfaction with academic or administrative programs or services.

4.8.4 *RefWorks*

RefWorks is a web-based bibliography and database manager that helps you create citations and reference lists for your writings. You can import references of books, articles, theses, dissertations, conference proceedings, etc. from online databases and other various sources into RefWorks and export them in the reference styles you choose (APA,MLA, Chicago, etc.) into Word or other types of documents.

Fig. 4.22 Link path to go to UM library research tools

4.8.5 Turnitin

Turnitin is a plagiarism prevention tool, which is designed to help faculty members to easily evaluate the originality of student's work by comparing their electronic documents to online sources and Turnitin-owned databases. Papers can now be accepted for checking in 30 different languages including Chinese (traditional and simplified), English and Portuguese (Fig. 4.22).

4.8.6 VeriGuide

VeriGuide is a plagiarism detection tool, which is developed by The Chinese University of Hong Kong and could help teaching staff for similarity detection, and readability assessment.

More information is available through UM library's homepage.

4.9 Citation

A citation is a way of giving credit to individuals for their creative and intellectual works that you utilized to support your research. It can also be used to locate particular sources. Proper citation is important for all scholarly work to avoid plagiarism. Typically, a citation can include the author's name, date, location of the publishing company, journal title, or DOI (Digital Object Identifier).

A citation style dictates the information necessary for a citation and how the information is ordered, as well as punctuation and other formatting.

There are many different ways of citing resources from your research. The citation style sometimes depends on the academic discipline involved. For example:

- APA (American Psychological Association) is used by Education, Psychology, and Sciences
- MLA (Modern Language Association) style is used by the Humanities
- Chicago/Turabian style is generally used by Business, History, and the Fine Arts
- IEEE style is used by engineering, computer science, and information technology.

Detailed introduction to different citation styles can be found in the discipline-specific units within this chapter and in Part III of this book.

Always consult with assignment or publication guidelines, etc. to determine what is required in your scholarly work.

References

Assignment Calculator (2018). http://library.umac.mo/html/services/reference/a_cal/main.asp. Accessed 26 Feb 2019

DeFelice B (ed) (1995) Science and engineering conference proceedings: a guide to sources for identification and verification. Association of College and Research Libraries, US

Guidelines for Interlibrary Loan/Document Delivery Service (2018). http://library.umac.mo/html/services/inter_loan/ref_ill_dds.html. Accessed 26 Feb 2019

Chapter 5
Information Literacy Resources in Science

Abstract This chapter is intended to help health science, medicine, engineering and information technology students quickly locate resources and reliable internet resources related to your study and research.

If your interest areas are health science, medicine, engineering, or technology, of some kind, you may find the following resources useful.

5.1 Health Science and Medicine

5.1.1 Reference Books

	Title: The Gale encyclopedia of medicine/Jacqueline L. Longe, editor (Electronic Resources) ISBN: 9781410317391 Ed. 5th Published: Farmington Hills, Mich.: Gale, Cengage Learning Year: 2015

(continued)

B. T. H. Leung et al., *Transferring Information Literacy Practices*,
https://doi.org/10.1007/978-981-13-7743-3_5

(continued)

	Title: Gale encyclopedia of medicine/Jacqueline L. Longe, editor; Deirdre S. Blanchfield, associate editor Location: 1/F A2 Reference Collection Status: LIB USE ONLY Call No. RC 41 Gal 2001 v.1 (~v.5) ISBN: 0787654892 Ed. 2nd Published: Detroit, MI: Gale Group Year: 2002
	Title: The Academic Medicine Handbook [electronic resource]: A Guide to Achievement and Fulfillment for Academic Faculty/edited by Laura Weiss Roberts [Electronic resource] ISBN: 9781461456933 Published: New York, NY: Springer New York: Imprint: Springer Year: 2013
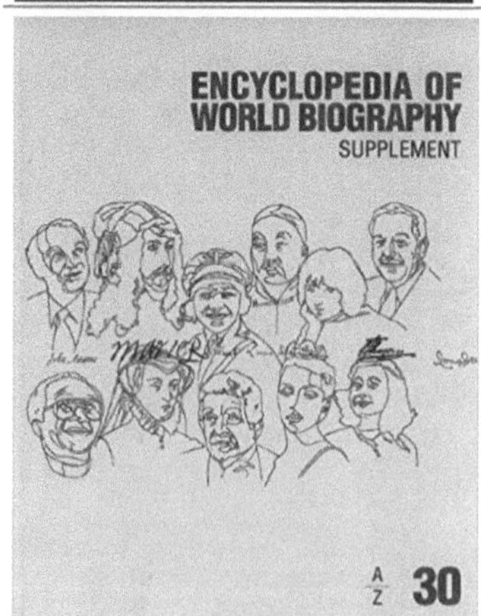	Title: Encyclopedia of world biography. Volume 30, Supplement [electronic resource] ISBN: 9781414462783 Ed. 2nd Published: Detroit, Mich.: Gale Year: c2009

(continued)

(continued)

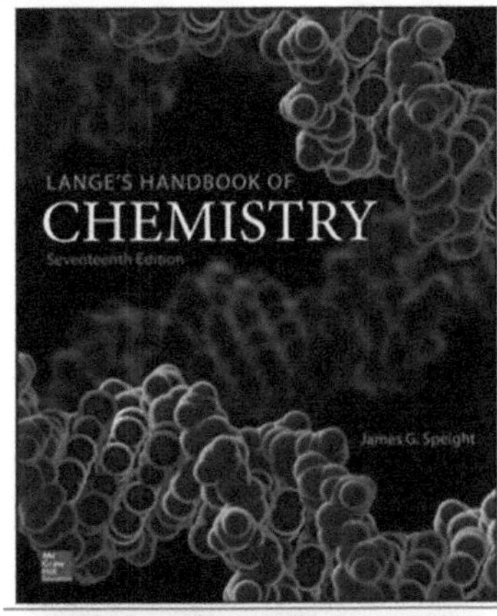 	Title: Lange's Handbook of Chemistry, Seventeenth Edition/James Speight [electronic resource]. ISBN: 9781259586101 Ed. 17th Published: New York, N.Y.: McGraw-Hill Education Year: 2016
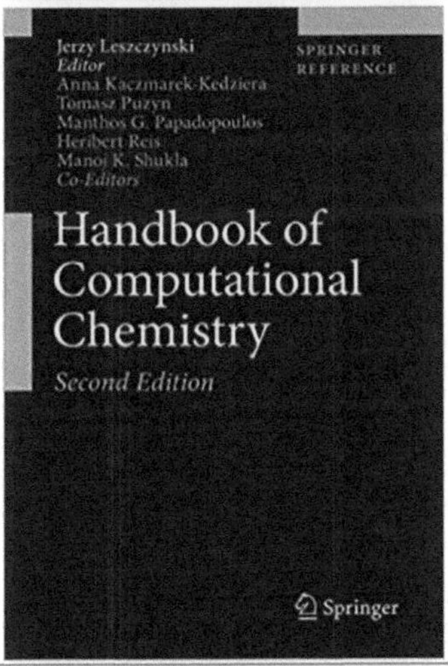 	Title: Handbook of Computational Chemistry [electronic resource]/edited by Jerzy Leszczynski, Anna Kaczmarek-Kedziera, Tomasz Puzyn, Manthos G. Papadopoulos, Heribert Reis, Manoj K. Shukla ISBN: 9783319272825 Ed. 2nd Published: Cham: Springer International Publishing: Imprint: Springer Year: 2017
 	Title: Encyclopedia of life sciences/Anne O'Daly, editor-in-chief Location: 1/F A2 Reference Collection Status: LIB USE ONLY Call No. QH 302.5 Enc v.1 (~v.11) ISBN: 0761402543 Published: New York: Marshall Cavendish Corp. Year: c1996

5.1.2 Featured Course Related Books

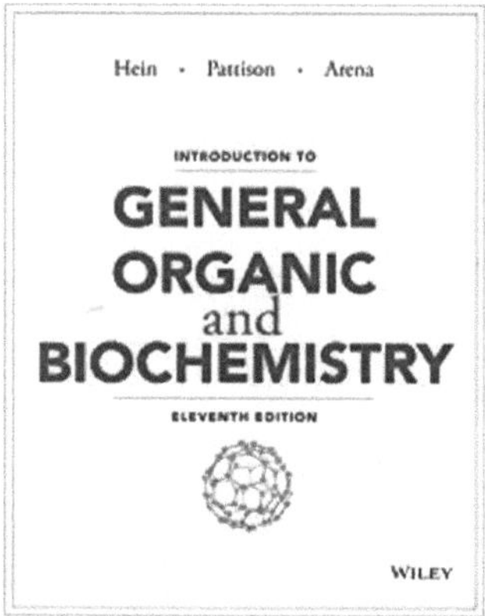	Title/Author: Introduction to general, organic, and biochemistry/Morris Hein, Mount San Antonio College, Scott Pattison, Ball State University, Susan Arena, University of Illinois, Urbana-Champaign Call No. QD 31.3 Hei 2015 ISBN: 9781118501894 Ed. 11th Publisher: Wiley Year: 2016
	Title/Author: Chemistry: The central science/Theodore L. Brown… [et al.] Call No. QD 31.3 Che 2015 ISBN: 9781292057712 Ed. 13th Publisher: Pearson Education Limited Year: 2015
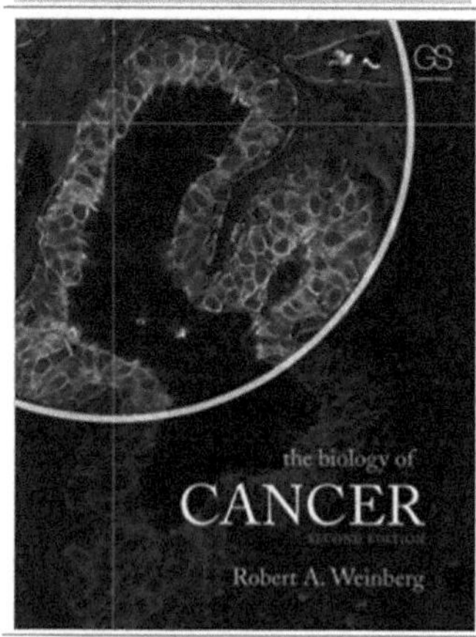	Title/Author: The biology of cancer/Robert A. Weinberg Call No. RC 268.4 Wei 2014 ISBN: 9780815342205 Ed. 2nd Publisher: Garland Science Year: 2014

(continued)

(continued)

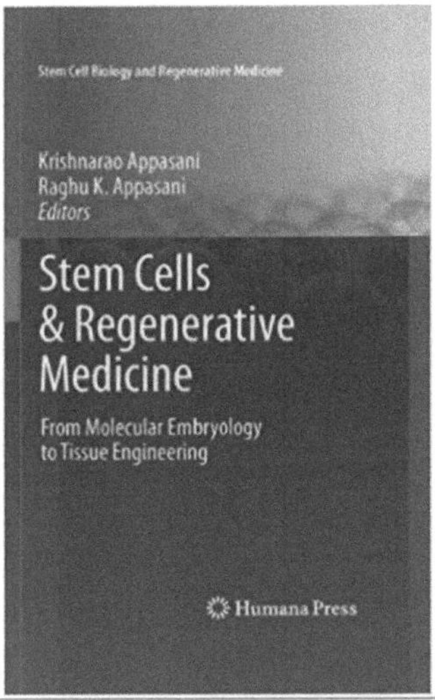	Title/Author: Stem Cells & Regenerative Medicine: From Molecular Embryology to Tissue Engineering/ edited by Krishnarao Appasani, Raghu K. Appasani Call No. QH 588 S83 Ste 2011 Course code: HSCI4002 Name of Lecturer: Prof. Ren-He Xu ISBN: 9781607618591 Ed. 1st Publisher: Humana Press Year: 2011
	Title/Author: 幹細胞與再生醫學/龐希甯 Call No. QH 588 S83 Kan 2014 ISBN: 9787117192422 Ed. 8 版 Publisher: 人民衛生出版社 Year: 2014
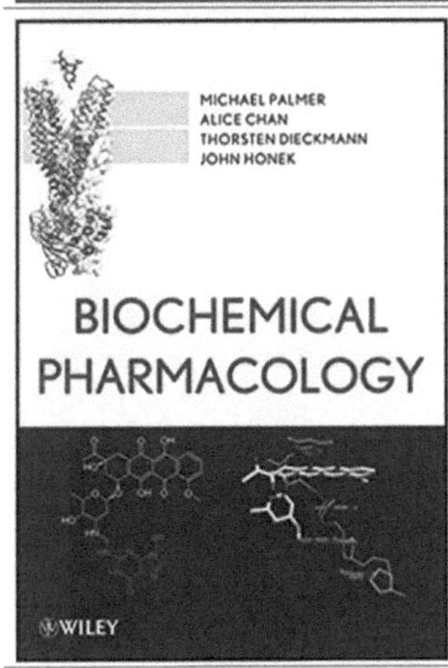	Title/Author: Biochemical phaomacology/Michael Palmer; with chapters by Alice Chan, Thorsten Dieckmann, John Hortek Call No. RM 300 Pal 2012 ISBN: 9780470174456 Ed. 1st Publisher: Wiley Year: 2012 therapeutically useful

(continued)

(continued)

	Title/Author: Pharmacology: Principles and practice/ edited by Miles Hacker, William Masser, Kenneth Bachmann Call No. RM 300 Pha 2009 ISBN: 9780123695215 Ed. 1st Publisher: Elsevier/Academic Press Year: 2017

5.1.3 Selected Books for Academic Writing

APA style is commonly used in the Health Sciences, but check with your Lecturer or Department to ensure you are using the correct style. APA style is based on the Publication manual of the American Psychological Association (6th ed).

5.1.4 Key Databases

- **PubMed**

PubMed comprises over 29 million citations for biomedical literature from MEDLINE, life science journals, and online books. PubMed citations and abstracts include the fields of biomedicine and health, covering portions of the life sciences, behavioral sciences, chemical sciences, and bioengineering. PubMed also provides access to additional relevant web sites and links to the other NCBI molecular biology resources (PubMed 2018).

- **Medline Complete**

MEDLINE Complete is the largest companion to the MEDLINE index and provides full text for over 2,400 medical journals not found with full text in any version of Academic Search, Health Source or Biomedical Reference Collection. In addition, MEDLINE Complete contains nearly 1,000 unique journals not found in MEDLINE with Full Text (MEDLINE Complete 2019).

- **Royal Society of Chemistry Journals**

This is an online platform from which you can access journal collection of biology, biophysics, chemical science, medicinal drug discovery and so on. With over 54,000 members and an international publishing and knowledge business, it is the UK's professional body for chemical scientists, supporting and representing their members and bringing together chemical scientists from all over the world (Royal Society of Chemistry Journals 2019).

- **Natural Product Updates**

Natural Product Updates is a literature alerting service keeping you current with recent developments in natural product chemistry. Covering a wide range of primary sources, Natural Product Updates topics include isolation of new natural products, biosynthesis, structure elucidation, synthesis and biological activity studies. Content is selected by our trained Editors. The updates include representative structures and are also searchable by topic, source organism, biological activity and structure type. Subscribers can set up personalized searches and receive alerts of the latest developments directly via email (Natural Product Updates 2019).

- **ProQuest Health and Medical Complete**

ProQuest Health and Medical Complete offers reliable, comprehensive journal coverage of clinical and biomedical topics, consumer health, health administration and more, it has in-depth coverage from over 1,500 publications with almost 1,300 available in full text and of these, over 900 include MEDLINE® indexing (ProQuest Health and Medical Complete 2019).

- **BioMed Central**

BioMed Central is an STM (Science, Technology and Medicine) publisher of 291 peer-reviewed open access journals. fA pioneer of open access publishing, BMC has an evolving portfolio of high quality peer-reviewed journals. These include broad interest titles such as BMC Biology and BMC Medicine, specialist journals such as Malaria Journal and Microbiome, and the BMC Series (BioMed Central 2019).

- **Chinese Medicinal Material Image Database**

Chinese Medicinal Material Images Database was developed by Hong Kong Baptist University Library and School of Chinese Medicine of Hong Kong Baptist University. It documents over 420 crude drugs commonly used in Chinese Medicine practice. The database provides drug information, such as annotated high quality photographs used to illustrate and identify key properties and selected microstructures (Chinese medicinal material image database 2013).

5.1.5 Selected Key Journals

- **Nature**

ISSN 0028-0836

Nature is a weekly international journal publishing the finest peer-reviewed research in all fields of science and technology on the basis of its originality, importance, interdisciplinary interest, timeliness, accessibility, elegance and surprising conclusions (Nature 2019).

- **Physics of Life Reviews**

ISSN 1571-0645

Physics of Life Reviews is an international journal appearing quarterly, that publishes review articles on physics of living systems, complex phenomena in biological systems, and so on (Physics of Life Reviews 2019).

- **PLOS Biology**

ISSN 1544-9173

PLOS Biology features works of exceptional significance, originality, and relevance in all areas of biological science, from molecules to ecosystems, including works at the interface of other disciplines, such as chemistry, medicine, and mathematics (PLoS Biology 2018).

- **BMC Biology**

ISSN 1741-7007

As the flagship biology journal of the BMC series, BMC Biology publishes outstanding research and commissioned content across all areas of biology (Biology 2019).

- **Chemical Reviews**

ISSN 0009-2665

Chemical Reviews is one of the most highly regarded and highest-ranked journals covering the general topic of chemistry (Chemical Reviews 2019).

- **Chemical Society Reviews**

ISSN 0306-0012

Chem Soc Rev (Chemical Society Reviews) is the Royal Society of Chemistry's leading reviews journal, publishing high-impact, succinct and reader-friendly articles at the forefront of the chemical sciences (Chemical Society Reviews 2019).

- **Nature Chemistry**

ISSN 1755-4330

Nature Chemistry is a monthly journal dedicated to publishing high-quality papers that describe the most significant and cutting-edge research in all areas of chemistry (Nature Chemistry 2019).

- **Value in Health**

ISSN 1098-3015

Value in Health contains original research articles for pharmacoeconomics, health economics, and outcomes research, as well as conceptual and health policy articles that provide valuable information for health care decision-makers (Value in Health 2019).

- **Health Affairs**

ISSN 0278-2715

Health Affairs is the leading journal of health policy thought and research. Its mission is to serve as a high-level, nonpartisan forum to promote analysis and discussion on improving health and health care, and to address such issues as cost, quality, and access (Health Affairs About Health Affairs 2019).

- **Journal of Health Economics**

ISSN 0167-6296

This journal seeks articles related to the economics of health and medical care (Journal of Health Economics 2019).

- **eLife**

ISSN 2050-084X

eLife is a non-profit organization inspired by research funders and led by scientists, it publishes work of the highest scientific standards and importance in all areas of the life and biomedical sciences (eLife 2019).

5.1.6 *Conference Proceedings in Health Sciences and Medicine*

- World congress on health medical informatics
- Annual symposium on computer applications in medical care transforming information changing health care
- European medical informatics conference
- Experimental biology meeting
- International meeting on chemical sensors
- International symposium on instrumentation science and technology
- International conference on biochemical analysis
- International conference on modern trends in activation analysis.

5.2 Science and Engineering/Technology Introduction

5.2.1 *Reference Books*

	Title/Author: ***Computer technology encyclopedia: quick reference for students and professionals*/Michael Graves** Call No. QA 76.15 Gra 2009 ISBN: 9781428322363 Ed. 1st Published: Clifton Park, N.Y.: Delmar Cengage Learning Year: c2009

(continued)

(continued)

	Title/Author: ***Encyclopedia of human computer interaction*/Claude Ghaoui** Location: 1/F A2 Reference Collection Status: LIB USE ONLY Call No. QA 76.9 H85 Enc ISBN: 1591405629 Published: Hershey PA: Idea Group Reference Year: c2006
	Title/Author: Encyclopedia of computer science/edited by Anthony Ralston, Edwin D. Reilly, David Hemmendinger Location: 1/F A2 Reference Collection Call No. QA 76.15 Enc 2000 Status: LIB USE ONLY Published: London: Nature Year: 2000
	Uniform Title: Encyclopedia of computer science and engineering. Chinese/ 計算機科學與工程百科全書 編譯委員會 Location: 1/F A2 Reference Collection Call No. QA 76.15 Enc 1991 ISBN: 7530802100 Status: LIB USE ONLY Published: 天津：天津科學技術 Year: 1991
No Book Cover	Anothony Ralston 主編的《Encyclopedia of Computer Science and Engineering》 (電腦科學與工程百科全書) 就是為此目的而編寫的。 撰稿人包括 300 多位學者, 其中不少人是電腦界的權威人士。 第一版於 1976 年出版。 本書是根據 1983 年增訂第二版翻譯的。

(continued)

(continued)

	Title/Author: McGraw-Hill personal computer programming encyclopedia: languages and operating systems/William J. Birnes, editor; Nancy Hayfield, production editor Location: 1/F A2 Reference Collection ISBN: 0070053898 Call No. QA76.6 MAC Status LIB USE ONLY Published: New York: McGraw-Hill Year: c1985
	Title/Author: Encyclopedia of environmental science and engineering/edited by James R. Pfafflin, Edward N. Ziegler Location: 1/F A2 Reference Collection ISBN: 2881245048 Call No. TD 9 Eny 1992 Status: LIB USE ONLY
	Title/Author: Wiley encyclopedia of electrical and electronics engineering/edited by John G. Webster Location: 1/F A2 Reference Collection ISBN: 0471139467 Call No. TK 9 Wil Status: LIB USE ONLY Published: New York: Wiley Year: c1999
	Title/Author: TCRC concise encyclopedia of mathematics/ Eric W. Weisstein Location: 1/F A2 Reference Collection ISBN: 1584883472 Call No. QA 5 Wei 2003 Status: LIB USE ONLY Published: Boca Raton: Chapman & Hall/CRC Year: c2003

(continued)

(continued)

	Title Encyclopedia of physics/edited by Rita G. Lerner, George L. Trigg. Location: 1/F A2 Reference Collection ISBN: 0895737523 Call No. QC5 ENC 1991 Status: LIB USE ONLY Published New York: VCH Year: c1991

5.2.2 *Selected Course Related Books*

	Title/Author: Numerical methods for engineers/Steven C. Chapra Call No. TA 345 Cha 2015 ISBN: 9780073397924 Ed. 7th Publisher: McGraw-Hill Education Year: 2015
	Title/Author: Computing essentials 2017: making IT work for you/Timothy J. O'Leary, Linda I. O'Leary, Danie A. O'Leary Call No. QA 76.5 O'L ISBN: 9781259921278 Ed. 26th Publisher: McGraw-Hill Education Year: 2017

(continued)

(continued)

	Title/Author: Pattern recognition/Sergios Theodoridis, Konstantinos Koutroumbas Call No. TK 7882 P3 The 2009 ISBN: 9781597492720 Ed. 4th Publisher: Academic Press Year: 2009
	Title/Author: Pattern classificaticn/Richard O. Duda, Peter E. Hart [and] David G. Stork Call No. Q 327 Dud 2001 ISBN: 9780471056690 Ed. 2nd Publisher: Wiley Year: 2001
	Title/Author: Vector mechanics for engineers. Dynamics/ Ferdinand P. Beer, E. Russell Johnston, Jr., Phillip J. Cornwell, Brian P. Self. Call No. TA 350 Bee 2016 ISBN: 9789814720045/9780077687342 Ed. 11th Publisher: McGraw-Hill Education Year: 2016

(continued)

(continued)

	Title/Author: Elements of environmental chemistry/Ronald A. Hites and Jonathan D. Raff Call No. TD 193 Hit 2012 ISBN: 9781118041550 Ed. 2nd Publisher: Wiley Year: 2012
	Title/Author: Principles of physics/Jearl Walker Call No. QC 21.3 Wal 2014 ISBN: 9781118230749 Ed. 10th Publisher: Wiley Year: 2014
	Title/Author: Engineering fundamentals of the internal combustion engine/Willard W. Pulkrabek Call No. TJ 785 Pul 2004 ISBN: 0131918559/0131405705 Ed. 2nd Publisher: Pearson/Prentice Hall Year: 2004

(continued)

(continued)

	Title/Author: Automotive mechanics/Ed May, Les Simpson Call No. TL 152 May 2010 ISBN: 9780070271876 (v.1), 9780070271883 (v.2) Ed. 8th Publisher: McGraw-Hill Year: 2010
	Title/Author: Automotive mechanics/William H. Crouse and Donald L. Anglin Call No. TL 205 Cro 1993 ISBN: 007112599X Ed. 10th Publisher: McGraw-Hill Year: 1993
	Title/Author: Mechanics of materials/Ferdinand P. Beer [and three others] Call No. TA 405 Bee 2015 ISBN: 9780073398235 Ed. 7th Publisher: McGraw-Hill Education Year: 2015
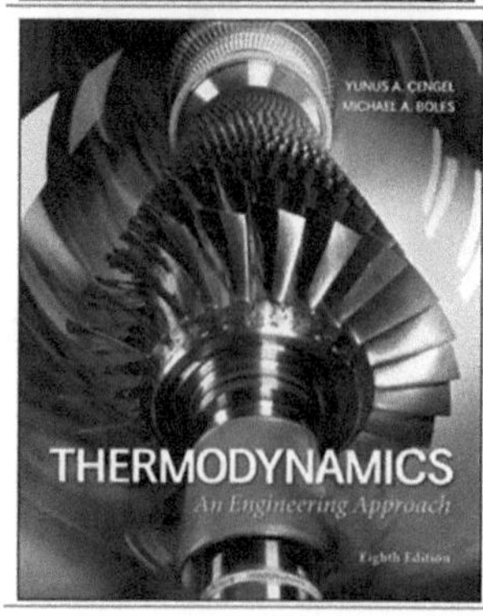	Title/Author: Thermodynamics: an engineering approach/ Yunus A. Cengel, Michael A. Boles Call No. TJ 265 Cen 2015 ISBN: 9780073398174 Ed. 8th Publisher: McGraw-Hill Education Year: 2015

(continued)

(continued)

<table>
<tr><td>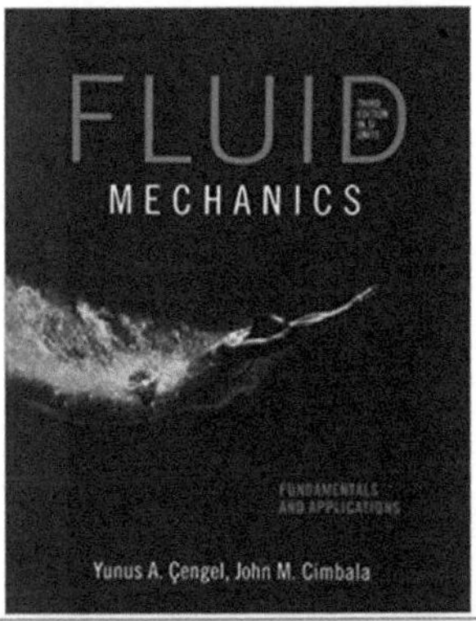
</td><td>Title/Author: Fluid mechanics: fundamentals and applications/Yunus A. Cengel, John M. Cimbala
Call No. TA 357 Cen 2014
ISBN: 9781259011221
Ed.
Publisher: McGraw-Hill Education
Year: 2014</td></tr>
<tr><td>
</td><td>Title/Author: A first course in the finite element method/ Daryl L. Logan, University of Wisconsin-Platteville
Call No. TA 347 F5 Log 2017
ISBN: 9781305637344
Ed. 6th
Publisher: Cengage
Year: 2017</td></tr>
<tr><td>
</td><td>Title/Author: Kinematics and dynamics of machinery/ Robert L. Norton
Call No. TJ 175 Nor 2013
ISBN: 9780071317092
Ed. 2nd ed. in SI units
Publisher: McGraw-Hill
Year: 2013</td></tr>
<tr><td></td><td>Title/Author: Calculus: early transcendentals/C. Henry Edwards, David E. Penney
Call No. QA 303.2 Edw 2014
ISBN: 9781292022178
Publisher: Pearson Education Limited
Year: 2014</td></tr>
</table>

(continued)

(continued)

	Title/Author: An introduction to the mathematics of money: saving and investing/David Lovelock, Mendel Marilou, A. Larry Wright. Call No. HG 4515.2 Lov 2007 ISBN: 9780387344324 Ed. 1st Publisher: Springer Year: 2007
	Title/Author: Basic stochastic processes: a course through exercises/Zdzislaw Brzezniak and Tomasz Zastawniak Call No. QA 274 Brz 1999 ISBN: 9783540761754 Ed. 1st Publisher: Springer Year: 2005

5.2.3 *Citing and Referencing*

The Institute of Electrical and Electronics Engineers (IEEE) citation style is now widely used in electrical, electronic and computing publications. IEEE provides instructions for authors for each type of publication such as journals, magazines, newsletters, and standards.

The three main parts of a reference are as follows:

- Author's name listed as first initial of first name, then full last.
- Title of article, patent, conference paper, etc., in quotation marks.
- Title of journal or book in italics.

The following examples demonstrate the format for some commonly used of electronic and print sources.

E-books

[1] L. Bass, P. Clements, and R. Kazman, *Software Architecture in Practice,* 2nd ed. Reading, MA: Addison Wesley, 2003. [E-book] Available: Safari e-book.

Journal Article in Scholarly Journal (published free of charge on the Internet)

[2] A. Altun, "Understanding hypertext in the context of reading on the web: Language learners' experience," *Current Issues in Education,* vol. 6, no. 12, July, 2005. [Online serial]. Available: http://cie.ed.asu.edu/volume6/number12/ [Accessed Dec. 2, 2007].

General Internet Site

[3] J. Geralds, "Sega Ends Production of Dreamcast," *vnunet.com*, para. 2, Jan 31, 2007. [Online]. Available: http://nli.vnunet.com/news/1116995. [Accessed Sept. 12, 2007].

Software

[4] Thomson ISI, *Endnote 7.* [CD-ROM]. Berkeley, CA: ISI ResearchSoft, 2006.

Books—Single Author

[5] W. K. Chen, *Linear Networks and Systems.* Belmont, CA: Wadsworth Press, 2003.

Books—Three or More Authors

[6] R. Hayes, G. Pisano, and S. Wheelwright, *Operations, Strategy, and Technical Knowledge.* Hoboken, NJ: Wiley, 2007.

Technical Report

[7] K. E. Elliott and C. M. Greene, "A local adaptive protocol," Argonne National Laboratory, Argonne, France, Tech. Report. 916-1010-BB, 7 Apr. 2007.

Patent/Standard

[8] K. Kimura and A. Lipeles, "Fuzzy controller component," U. S. Patent 14, 860,040, 14 Dec 2006.

Article in Journal (paginated by annual volume)

[9] K. A. Nelson, R. J. Davis, D. R. Lutz, and W. Smith, "Optical generation of tunable ultrasonic waves," *Journal of Applied Physics,* vol. 53, no. 2, Feb., pp. 1144-1149, 2002.

Article in Professional Journal (paginated by issue)

[10] J. Attapangittya, "Social studies in gibberish," *Quarterly Review of Doublespeak,* vol. 20, no. 1, pp. 9–10, 2003.

Please note this style guide is wide ranging, you are highly suggested to refer to IEEE reference guide for the detailed way to identify all sources. IEEE also provides more information and tools on its website for authors, such as video tutorials, publication recommender, article templates, graphics analyzer, LaTex analyzer and reference preparation assistant, etc. Please visit IEEE author center at ieee.org for the details.

5.2.4 *Key Databases*

- **IEEE Xplore**

The IEEE Xplore digital library is a powerful resource for discovery of scientific and technical content published by the IEEE (Institute of Electrical and Electronics Engineers) and its publishing partners.

IEEE Xplore provides web access to more than four-million full-text documents from some of the world's most highly-cited publications in electrical engineering, computer science, and electronics (xplore 2019).

- **Computer database (GALE)**

Computer Database provides access to leading business and technical publications in the computer, telecommunications, and electronics industries. The database includes more than 600 journals and periodicals, providing information on computer-related product introductions, news and reviews in areas such as hardware, software, electronics, engineering, communications, and the application of technology. Exclusive features, including Topic Finder, InterLink, and a mobile-optimized interface, support and enhance the search experience [Computer database (GALE) 2019].

- **ACM Portal: The ACM digital library**

The ACM Digital Library (DL) is the world's most comprehensive database of full-text articles and bibliographic literature covering computing and information technology. This renowned repository includes the complete collection of ACM publications plus an extended bibliographic database of core works in computing from scholarly publishers (ACM Portal: The ACM digital library 2019).

- **Computers and Applied Science Complete**

It covers the research and development spectrum of the computing and applied sciences disciplines, and provides indexing and abstracts for more than 1,470 academic journals, professional publications, and other reference sources from a diverse collection. Full text is also available for more than 660 periodicals (Computers and Applied Science Complete 2019).

- **ProQuest Computing**

This database is a premium resource for those who need access to comprehensive coverage of computer topics. The database includes numerous titles, most of them in full text, allowing users to search records dating back to the early 1990s (Computing Database 2019).

- **AccessEngineering**

AccessEngineering is an award-winning engineering reference tool for professionals, academics, and students that provides seamless access to the world's best-known, most-used collection of authoritative, regularly updated engineering reference information. AccessEngineering also comprises dynamic online features, such as instructional, faculty made videos, calculators, interactive tables and charts, as well as personalization tools allowing users to organize crucial project information as they work (Access Engineering 2019).

- **Engineering Village (Former Name: Compendex)**

Engineering Village has the search, analytics, and navigation tools that engineers need to efficiently generate research, assess the impact and relevancy of critical information, and discover new insights for addressing the world's toughest engineering challenges. All content and features are designed for engineers, so results and outcomes are always engineering-relevant. [Engineering Village (Former Name: Compendex) 2019].

- **INSPEC**

This bibliographic database provides abstracts and indexing to the world's scientific and technical papers in physics, electrical engineering, electronics, communications, control engineering, computing, information technology, manufacturing, production and mechanical engineering (INSPEC 2014).

- **arXiv**

Open access to 1,502,407 e-prints in the fields of physics, mathematics, computer science, quantitative biology, quantitative finance, statistics, electrical engineering and systems science, and economics. Submissions to arXiv should conform to Cornell University academic standards. arXiv is owned and operated by Cornell University, a private not-for-profit educational institution. arXiv is funded by Cornell University, the Simons Foundation and by the member institutions (arXiv 2019).

- **MathSciNet**

MathSciNet® is an electronic publication offering access to a carefully maintained and easily searchable database of reviews, abstracts and bibliographic information for much of the mathematical sciences literature. Over 100,000 new items are added each year, most of them classified according to the Mathematics Subject Classification (MathSciNet 2019).

- **American Physical Society Journals**

The American Physical Society (APS) is a professional organization of physicists. This database provides access to the most recent information available through all APS journals, including those in PROLA and Physical Review Focus, an online index, society news and events, and articles scheduled for upcoming issues (Physical 2019).

- **ProQuest Telecommunications**

This database is an essential resource for anyone researching the industry or its technology. Whether you're looking for the latest news on WAP technology, following market penetration of new technologies, or gathering information about the key players in this field, ProQuest Telecommunications helps you stay one step ahead. The database includes over 140 titles, with more than 115 available in full text. Search more than 600,000 records, dating back to the early 1990s (Telecommunications Database 2019).

5.2.5 Top Journals

- **International Journal of Computer Vision**

ISSN: 0920-5691 (Print) 1573-1405 (Online)

International Journal of Computer Vision (IJCV) details the science and engineering of this rapidly growing field. Regular articles present major technical advances of broad general interest. Survey articles offer critical reviews of the state of the art and/or tutorial presentations of pertinent topics (International Journal of Computer Vision 2012).

- **IEEE Industrial Electronics Magazine**

ISSN: 1932-4529

IEEE Industrial Electronics Magazine publishes peer-reviewed articles that present emerging trends and practices in industrial electronics product research and development, key insights, and tutorial surveys in the field of interest to the membership of the IEEE Industrial Electronics Society (Magazine 2019).

- **ACTA Numerica**

ISSN: 0962-4929 (Print), 1474-0508 (Online)

Acta Numerica is the top-cited journal for the last two years in MathSciNet. Its annual collection of review articles includes survey papers by leading researchers in numerical analysis and scientific computing (Numerica 2019).

- **IEEE Transactions on Pattern Analysis and Machine Intelligence**

ISSN: 0162-8828

The IEEE Transactions on Pattern Analysis and Machine Intelligence (TPAMI) is published monthly. Its editorial board strives to present most important research results in areas within TPAMI's scope (Analysis and Intelligence 2018).

- **Proceedings of the IEEE**

ISSN: 0018-9219

Proceedings of the IEEE is the leading journal to provide in-depth review, survey, and tutorial coverage of the technical developments in electronics, electrical and computer engineering, and computer science (Proceedings of the IEEE 2019).

- **IEEE Transactions on Cloud Computing**

ISSN: 2168-7161

The IEEE Transactions on Cloud Computing (TCC) is a scholarly journal dedicated to the multidisciplinary field of cloud computing (Computing 2019).

- **Automatica**

ISSN: 0005-1098

A Journal of IFAC, the International Federation of Automatic Control, Automatica is a leading archival publication in the field of systems and control (Automatica 2014).

- **Annals of Mathematics**

ISSN: 0003-486X

The Annals of Mathematics is a bimonthly mathematical journal published by Princeton University and the Institute for Advanced Study (Annals of Mathematics 2019).

- **Journal of Information Technology**

ISSN: 0268-3962

The Journal of Information Technology (JIT) is a top-ranked journal in its field, focused on new research addressing technology and the management of IT - including strategy, change, infrastructure, human resources, sourcing, system development and implementation, communications, technology developments, technology futures, national policies and standards, as well as articles that advance understanding and application of research approaches and methods (Journal of Information Technology 2012).

- **IEEE Systems Journal**

ISSN: 1932-8184

The IEEE Systems Journal (ISJ) is the technical journal of the IEEE Systems Council, and is published quarterly (Journal 2019).

- **Internet Research**

ISSN: 1066-2243

Internet Research (INTR) is a peer-reviewed academic journal, published by Emerald Publishing. It aims to describe, assess and foster understanding of the role of wide-area, multi-purpose computer networks such as the Internet (Internet Research 2019).

- **Artificial Intelligence Review**

ISSN 0269-2821

Artificial Intelligence Review publishes state-of-the-art research reports and critical evaluations of applications, techniques and algorithms in artificial intelligence, cognitive science and related disciplines. It serves as a forum for the work of researchers and application developers from these fields (Artificial Intelligence Review 2012).

5.2.6 *Conference Proceeding in Science and Engineering/ Technology*

- IEEE international conference on system man and cybernetics
- ASEE annual conference
- IEEE RSJ international conference on intelligent robots and systems

- International joint conference on neural networks
- ASME international mechanical engineering congress and exposition
- IEEE international symposium on circuits and systems
- IEEE wireless communications and networking conference
- International conference on numerical analysis and applied mathematics
- IEEE conference on decision and control.

References

Access Engineering (2019) About. https://www.accessengineeringlibrary.com/about. Accessed 07 Mar 2019

Health Affairs. About health affairs. https://www.healthaffairs.org/about. Accessed 07 Mar 2019

ACM Portal: The ACM digital library (2019) ACM digital library. https://www.acm.org/publications/digital-library. Accessed 07 Mar 2019

IEEE Transactions on Pattern Analysis and Machine Intelligence (2018) undefined—undefined | IEEE Computer Society Digital Library. https://www.computer.org/csdl/journal/tp/misc/14403. Accessed 07 Mar 2019

Annals of Mathematics (2019) Wikipedia. https://en.wikipedia.org/wiki/Annals_of_Mathematics. Accessed 07 Mar 2019

Artificial Intelligence Review (2012) Springer. https://link.springer.com/journal/10462. Accessed 07 Mar 2019

arXiv (2019) arXiv.org e-Print archive. https://arbeiten-und-sparen.info/out_arXiv.org. Accessed 07 Mar 2019

Automatica (2014) A journal of IFAC—the international federation of automatic control. http://www.autsubmit.com/editormessages.html. Accessed 07 Mar 2019

BMC Biology (2019) Springer. https://link.springer.com/journal/12915. Accessed 05 Mar 2019

BioMed Central (2019) BMC, research in progress. https://www.biomedcentral.com/. Accessed 05 Mar 2019

Chemical Reviews (2019) About the journal. https://pubs.acs.org/page/chreay/about.html. Accessed 05 Mar 2019

Chemical Society Reviews (2019) Chemical society reviews. http://www.rsc.org/journals-books-databases/about-journals/chem-soc-rev/. Accessed 05 Mar 2019

Chinese medicinal material image database (2013) 中藥材圖像數據庫. https://library.hkbu.edu.hk/electronic/libdbs/mmd/. Accessed 05 Mar 2019

Computer database (GALE) (2019) Computer database. https://www.gale.com/intl/c/computer-database. Accessed 07 March 2019

Computers & Applied Science Complete (2019) EBSCO. https://www.ebsco.com/products/research-databases/computers-applied-sciences-complete. Accessed 07 March 2019

IEEE Transactions on Cloud Computing (2019) IEEE xplore: IEEE transactions on cloud computing—(Current Issue). https://ieeexplore.ieee.org/xpl/mostRecentIssue.jsp?punumber=6245519&filter=issueId%20EQ%20%226562694%22&pageNumber=4. Accessed 07 Mar 2019

Computing Database (2019) About computing database. https://search.proquest.com/computing/productfulldescdetail?accountid=12206. Accessed 07 Mar 2019

eLife (2019) Biocuration 2019. https://www.biocuration2019.org/eLife. Accessed 07 Mar 2019

Engineering Village (Former Name: Compendex) (2019) Features—engineering village | Elsevier. https://www.elsevier.com/solutions/engineering-village/features. Accessed 07 Mar 2019

INSPEC (2014) University of Macau—Wu Yee Sun Library. https://library.umac.mo/html/databases/e_databases_id_res.asp?getsuid=19. Accessed 07 Mar 2019

International Journal of Computer Vision (2012) Springer. https://link.springer.com/journal/11263. Accessed 07 Mar 2019
Internet Research (2019) Wikipedia. https://en.wikipedia.org/wiki/Internet_Research_(journal). Accessed 07 Mar 2019
IEEE Systems Journal (2019) IEEE systems council. https://www.ieeesystemscouncil.org/publication/systems-journal. Accessed 07 Mar 2019
Journal of Health Economics. Journal of health economics-Elsevier. https://www.journals.elsevier.com/journal-of-health-economics. Accessed 07 Mar 2019
Journal of Information Technology (2012) Springer. https://link.springer.com/journal/41265. Accessed 07 Mar 2019
IEEE Industrial Electronics Magazine (2019) IEEE Xplore: IEEE Industrial Electronics Magazine. https://ieeexplore.ieee.org/xpl/RecentIssue.jsp?punumber=4154573. Accessed 07 Mar 2019
MathSciNet (2019) MR: About MathSciNet. https://mathscinet.ams.org/mathscinet/help/about.html?version=2. Accessed 07 Mar 2019
MEDLINE Complete (2019) Full-Text biomedical database. https://health.ebsco.com/products/medline-complete. Accessed 05 Mar 2019
Natural Product Updates (2019) Natural product updates. http://pubs.rsc.org/lus/natural-product-updates/. Accessed 05 Mar 2019
Nature (2019) About the Journal Nature. https://www.nature.com/nature/about. Accessed 05 Mar 2019
Nature Chemistry (2019) About the journal | Nature Chemistry. https://www.nature.com/nchem/about. Accessed 07 Mar 2019
ACTA Numerica (2019) Number theory—Cambridge University Press. http://www.cambridgecloudflare.org/browse/browse_journals.asp?subjectid=1010184. Accessed 07 Mar 2019
APS Physical (2019) APS Home. https://www.aps.org/. Accessed 07 Mar 2019
Physics of Life Reviews (2019) Journal-Elsevier. https://www.journals.elsevier.com/physics-of-life-reviews. Accessed 05 Mar 2019
PLoS Biology (2018) navia ia-module tiles. https://archive.org/details/plosbiology&tab=collection. Accessed 05 Mar 2019
Proceedings of the IEEE (2019) IEEE xplore. https://ieeexplore.ieee.org/xpl/RecentIssue.jsp?punumber=5. Accessed 07 Mar 2019
ProQuest Health and Medical Complete (2019) BHM regional library. https://bhmlib.org/health-medical/. Accessed 05 Mar 2019
PubMed (2018) Home. https://www.ncbi.nlm.nih.gov/pubmed/. Accessed 05 Mar 2019
Royal Society of Chemistry Journals (2019) About the Royal Society of Chemistry. http://www.rsc.org/about-us/. Accessed 05 Mar 2019
Telecommunications Database (2019) ProQuest. https://search.proquest.com/telecomms?accountid=17200. Accessed 07 Mar 2019
Value in Health (2019) Value in Health—Journal—Elsevier. https://www.journals.elsevier.com/value-in-health. Accessed 07 Mar 2019
IEEE xplore (2019) About IEEE xplore. https://ieeexplore.ieee.org/xpl/aboutUs.jsp. Accessed 07 Mar 2019

Chapter 6
Information Literacy Resources in the Social Sciences

Abstract This chapter is intended to help arts and humanities, business and management, education, law and social science students quickly locate resources and reliable internet resources related to your study and research.

6.1 Arts and Humanities

This section has been developed to assist in locating and using featured print and online resources of art and humanities subject of the UM library. It contains a variety of resources for study, research and teaching.

6.1.1 Reference Books

	Title: 華僑華人百科全書. 文學藝術卷 = Encyclopedia of Chinese overseas. Volume of literature & art/ <<華僑華人百科全書>> 編輯委員會編輯 Location: 1/F A2 Reference Collection Call No. DS 732 Hua v.11 ISBN: 7801203046 Published: 北京市: 中國華僑出版社 Year: 2000

(continued)

B. T. H. Leung et al., *Transferring Information Literacy Practices*,
https://doi.org/10.1007/978-981-13-7743-3_6

(continued)

	Title: Encyclopedia of drawing art and painting [electronic resource]/Alfonzo Broyles, Velma Cain ISBN: 9788132310952 Published: Delhi, India: College Publishing House Year: 2012
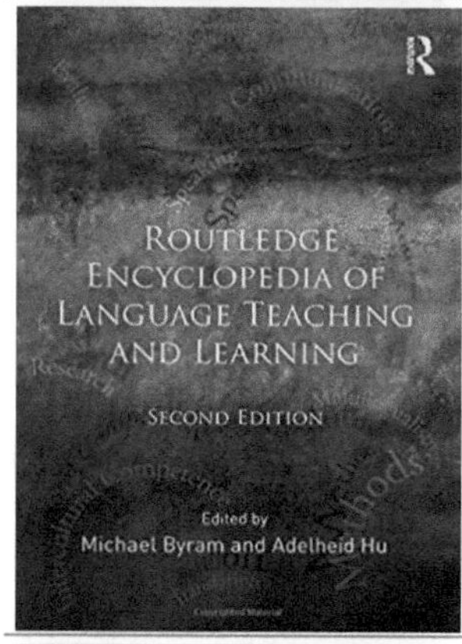	Title: Routledge encyclopedia of language teaching and learning/edited by Michael Byram and Adelheid Hu Location: 1/F A2 Reference Collection Call No. P 51 Rou 2013 ISBN: 9780415593762 Ed. 2nd Published: Abingdon, Oxon: Routledge Year: 2013
	Title: Routledge encyclopedia of second language acquisition/edited by Peter Robinson Location: 2/F C3 Language & Literature Call No. P 118.2 Rou 2013 ISBN: 9780415877510 Published: New York; London: Routledge Year: 2013

(continued)

(continued)

	Title: The Cambridge encyclopedia of the language sciences/edited by Patrick Colm Hogan Location: 1/F A2 Reference Collection Call No. P 29 Cam 2011 ISBN: 9780521866897 Published: Cambridge; New York: Cambridge University Press Year: 2011
	Title: Encyclopedia of philosophy [electronic resource]/ Donald M. Borchert, editor in chief ISBN: 9780028660721 Ed. 2nd Published: Detroit, Mich.: Macmillan Reference USA Year: c2006
	Title: The Routledge handbook of language and media/ edited by Colleen Cotter and Daniel Perrin ISBN: 9781315673134 Published: Milton Park, Abingdon, Oxon; New York, NY: Routledge Year: 2018

(continued)

(continued)

	Title: The Routledge handbook of language and politics/ edited by Ruth Wodak and Bernhard Forchtner ISBN: 9781315183718 Published: Milton Park, Abingdon, Oxon; New York, NY: Routledge Year: 2018
	Title: Encyclopedic dictionary of applied linguistics: a handbook for language teaching/edited by Keith Johnson and Helen Johnson Location: 1/F A2 Reference Collection Call No. P 129 Enc ISBN: 0631180893 Published: Oxford, UK; Malden, USA: Blackwell Year: 1998 (1999 printing)
	Title: A handbook to literature/by C. Hugh Holman Location: 2/F C3 Language & Literature Ed. 4th Call No. PN 41 Hol 1980 ISBN: 0672614413 Published: Indianapolis: Bobbs-Merrill Education Pub. Year: c1980

6.1.2 Featured Course Related Books

Title/Author: Understanding second language acquisition/ Lourdes Ortega
Call No. P 118.2 Ort 2013
ISBN: 9780340905593
Ed. 1st
Publisher: Routledge
Year: 2013

Title/Author: The grammar book: form, meaning, and use for English language teachers/Diane Larsen-Freeman [and four others]
Call No. PE 1128 A2 Lar 2016
ISBN: 9781111351861
Ed. 3rd
Publisher: Heinle Cengage Learning
Year: 2015

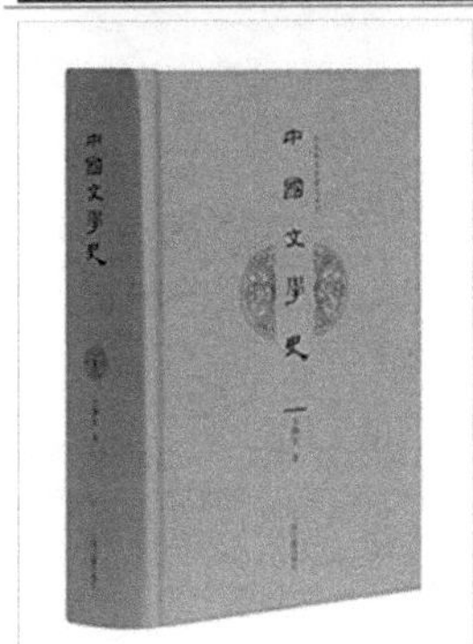

Title/Author: 中國文學史/台靜農
Call No. PL 2264 Tai 2017
ISBN: 9787532583553
Ed. Print book
Publisher: 上海古籍出版社
Year: 2017

(continued)

(continued)

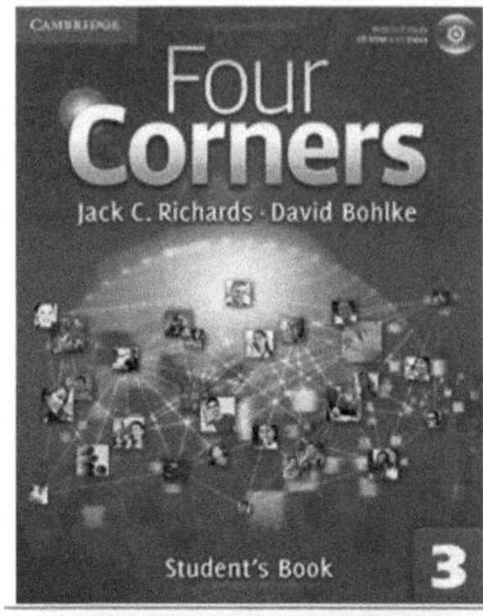	Title/Author: Four Comers Level 3 student's book with self-study CD ROM/Jack C. Richards, David Bohlke Call No. PE 1128 Ric 2012 ISBN: 9780521127554 Ed. n/a Publisher: Cambridge University Press Year: 2011
	Title/Author: Keynote. Intermediate: student's book/Paul Dummett, John Hughes, Helen Stephenson Call No. PE 1128 Dum 2016 ISBN: 9781305399099 Ed. Publisher: National Geographic Learning Year: 2016
	Title/Author: The Norton anthology of English literature, the major authors/Stephen Greenblatt, general editor Call No. PR 1109 Nor 2013 ISBN: 9780393919639 Ed. 9th Publisher: W. W. Norton & Co. Year: 2013

(continued)

(continued)

	Title/Author: The study of language/George Yule Call No. P 107 Yul 2017 ISBN: 9781316606759 Ed. 6th Publisher: Cambridge University Press Year: 2017
	Title/Author: Studio (Translation and interpreting studies 2019): Das Deutschbuch Al. l: Deutsch als Fremdsprache/ herausgegeben von Hermann Funk, im Auftrag des Verlages erarbeitet von Hermann Funk und Christina Kuhn; Ubungen, Laura NieLsen and Kerstin Rische; Phonetik, Beate Lex. Sowie Beate Redecker Call No. PF 3066 Stu 2013 ISBN: 9783065205306 Ed. 1st Publisher: Comelsen Year: 2013
	Title/Author: Foe/J. M. Coetzee Call No. PR 9369.3 C58 Foe 1987 ISBN: 9780241950111/9780140110326 Ed. UK Edition Publisher: Penguin Year: 1987

(continued)

(continued)

	Title/Author: A handbook of critical approaches to literature/Wilfred L. Guerin … [et al.] Call No. PN 81 Han 2004 ISBN: 7560041531 Ed. 1st Publisher: Oxford UP/Foreign Language Teaching and Research (Shanghai) Year: 1999
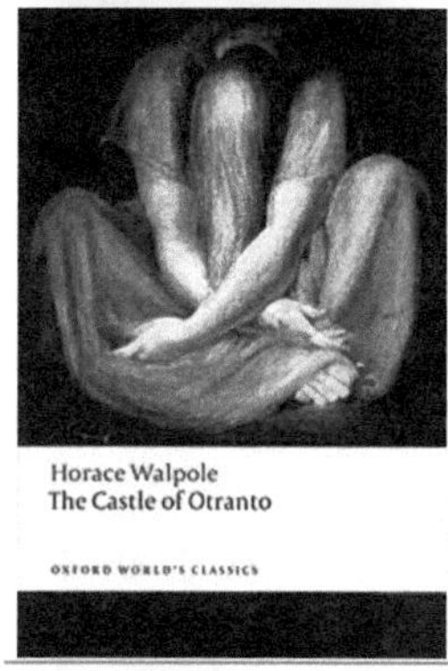	Title/Author: The castle of Otranto: a gothic story/edited with an introduction and notes by Nick Groom Call No. PR 3757 W2 Cal 2014 ISBN: 9780198704447 Ed. 1st Publisher: Oxford University Press Year: 2014
	Title/Author: Northanger abbey; Lady Susan; The Watsons and Sanditon/Jane Austen; edited by James Kinsley and John Davie, with an introduction by Claudia L. Johnson Call No. PR 4034 N6 Nor 2003 ISBN: 9780199535545 Ed. 1st Publisher: Oxford University Press Year: 2008

(continued)

(continued)

	Title/Author: The monk/Matthew Lewis; edited by Howard Anderson; with an introduction and notes by Emma McEvoy Call No. PR 4887 Mon 1998 ISBN: 9780199535682 Ed. 1st Publisher: Oxford University Press Year: 2008
	Title/Author: Echo: methode de francais. A1/J. Girardet, J. Pecheur avec la collaboration de C. Gibbe Call No. PC 2129 Gir 2013 ISBN: 9782090385885 Ed. 2nd Publisher: CLE International/Sejer Year: 2013
	Title/Author: Sex Matters: The Sexuality and Society Reader/Mindy Stobler Call No. HQ 16 Sex 2014 ISBN: 9780393935868 Ed. 4th Publisher: W. W. Norton and Company Year: 2013

(continued)

(continued)

	Title/Author: The moral life: an introductory reader in ethics and literature/Louis P. Pojman, Lewis Vaughn Call No. BJ 1012 Poj 2014 ISBN: 9780199950850 Ed. 5th Publisher: Oxford University Press Year: 2014
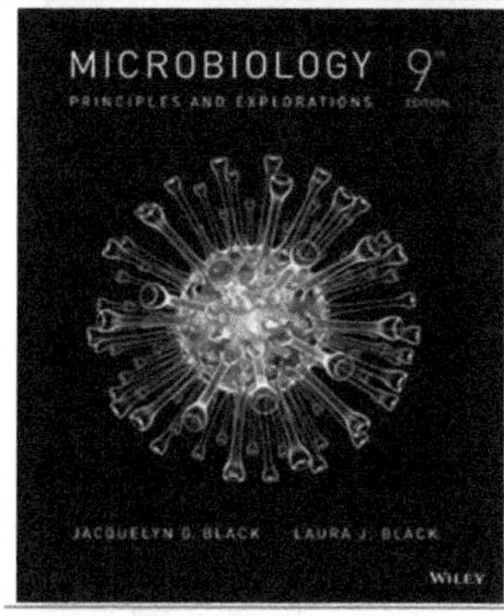	Title/Author: Microbiology: principles and explorations/ Jacquelyn G. Black, Marymount University, Arlington, Virginia and Laura J. Black Call No. QR 41.2 Bla 2015 ISBN: 9781118743164 Ed. 9th Publisher: John Wiley & Sons Year: 2014
	Title/Author: 大家的日本語 . 初級I/[編著者: スリーエーネットワーク] Call No. PL 539.3 Min 2015 Course code: JAPN1004 Name of Lecturer: Dr. QingZhen Deng ISBN: 9789863210870 Ed. 改訂版 Publisher: 大新書局 Year: 2015

6.1.3 Academic Writing and Citation Resources

MLA (Modern Language Association) citation style used in literature and the humanities. The MLA system uses in-text citations rather than footnotes or endnotes. The citations in-text are very brief, usually just the author's family name and a relevant page number. These citations correspond to the full references in the list of works cited at the end of the document.

Detailed information, instructions and examples can be found in the following two books.

	Title: MLA handbook for writers of research papers. Chinese ISBN: 9575867629 Published: 臺北：書林 Year: 1998
Modern Language Association MLA	MLA International Bibliography from Gale [Electronic Resources]

6.1.4 Key Databases

- **America: History and Life**

America: History and Life is the definitive index of literature covering the history and culture of the United States and Canada from prehistory to the present. Indexing hundreds of journals, it is an invaluable bibliographic database for history students (America: History and Life 2019).

- **Art and humanities citation index (A&HCI)**

Arts and Humanities Citation Index is a multidisciplinary index to scholarly journal literature in the arts and humanities. It indexes individually selected, relevant items from major arts and humanities journals. Full-text is only available to those e-journals to which the Library has subscribed [Art and humanities citation index (A&HCI) 2014].

- **China and Modern World**

China and the Modern World is a multi-module digitization and publishing program that documents China's transformation from an imperial dynasty into a modern republic. Consisting of monographs, manuscripts, periodicals, correspondence and letters, photos, and other kinds of historical documents, these collections provide excellent primary source material for the understanding and research of the various aspects of China during the nineteenth and twentieth centuries (China and Modern World 2014).

- **China: Culture and Society**

The core of China: Culture and Society is the pamphlets held in the Charles W. Wason Collection on East Asia housed in the Carl A. Kroch Library of Cornell University. Mostly in English and published between c. 1750 and 1929, and amounting to around 1,200 items in 220 bound volumes, these rare pamphlets form part of one of the deepest and most extensive collections of literature on China and the Chinese in the Western world and constitute a rich resource for scholars and teachers in numerous disciplines.

The pamphlets have all been digitised in colour and are full-text searchable. Many are illustrated and feature lavish cover art (China: Culture and Society 2014).

- **Films on demand**

Films Media Group is the premier source of high-quality video on academic, vocational, and life-skills topics for schools, colleges, libraries, the medical community, and other institutions. It offers thousands of educational videos, many exclusive, from top producers including Films for the Humanities and Sciences and hundreds more. Available formats include DVD and streaming video (Films on demand 2014).

- **Historical reproduction**

Historical Reproduction is a collection of rare documents and newspapers in Chinese and English languages traced back to the 15th Century. It was collected from various sources worldwide, converted to digital images from printed documents, microfilms, microfiches and etc. Please find your interested title below and access by clicking. Most of the access of Collection is restricted to eligible Library users only (Historical reproduction 2014).

- **Web Gallery of art**

The Web Gallery of Art is a virtual museum and searchable database of European fine arts from the 3rd to 19th centuries. It was started in 1996 as a topical site of Renaissance art, originated in the Italian city-states of the 14th century and spread to other countries in the 15th and 16th centuries. Intending to present Renaissance art as comprehensively as possible, the scope of the collection was later extended to show its medieval roots as well as its evolution to Baroque and Rococo via Mannerism. Encouraged by the feedback from the visitors, sections for decorative arts and architecture were set up and the scope of the collection was extended to include Early Christian and Pre-Romanesque art and architecture of the 3rd-10th centuries. 19th-century art was also included (Web Gallery of art 2019).

- **澳門大學圖書館古籍特藏圖錄**

> 《圖錄》收錄了大學館藏中的 100 種精品古籍，一定程度上揭示了大學館藏的特色及珍貴的古籍特藏；全書由“歷代名著”、“鄉邦文獻”及“宗教譯述”三部份內容組成。《圖錄》爲澳門大學成立二十五周年銀禧獻禮。

(澳門大學圖書館古籍特藏圖錄 2014).

- **Early English books online**

Following its first launch in 1998, EEBO now contains page images of virtually every work printed in England, Ireland, Scotland, Wales and British North America and works in English printed elsewhere from 1473–1700. More than 200 libraries worldwide have contributed to EEBO (Early English books online 2019).

- **Fonte Academica**

It is a collection of over 330 scholarly journals from Brazil and Portugal. All major subject areas are covered with particular emphasis on agriculture, biological sciences, economics, history, law, literature, medicine, philosophy, psychology, public administration, religion and sociology. It is a rapidly growing collection of journals from Brazil and Portugal designed to make academic research readily available in PDF format (Fonte Academica 2014).

- **Fuente Academica**

It offers more than 505 scholarly journals from Latin America, Portugal and Spain. All major subject areas are covered with particular emphasis on agriculture, biological sciences, economics, history, law, literature, philosophy, psychology, public administration, religion and sociology (Fuente Academica 2014).

- **Literature online**

Literature Online is the leading online resource for the study and teaching of literature in English. It is a fully integrated service that combines the texts of over 355,000 literary works with a vast library of key criticism and reference resources. Literature Online's collection of accurate poetry, prose and drama is relied upon by researchers around the world on a daily basis and the essential criticism and reference resources, including an ever-growing library of full-text journals and author biographies, helps keep you up to date on the latest research into every aspect of literary and linguistic study (Literature online 2014).

- **國學寶典**

> 《國學寶典數據庫》是一套面向中文圖書館、中國文化研究機構、專業研究人員和文史愛好者的中華古籍全文資料檢索系統。收錄上起先秦、下至民國兩千多年的所有用漢字作爲載體的歷代典籍，幷收錄了清代至當代學者對相關古籍研究的重要成果。該數據庫中收錄典籍均爲文史研究人員常用資料，具有極強的實用價值。

(國學寶典 2014).

- **Philosopher's Index**

This bibliographic database covers scholarly research in all major fields of philosophy. A thorough index of journal literature, it features author-written abstracts covering scholarly research published in journals and books (Philosopher's Index 2014).

- **Books on China online**

This database consists of books in Western languages on China published during 18th to early 20th Century. It covers the subject areas of history, religion, international relations, language and literature, social life and so on (Books on China online 2019).

- **Translation studies bibliography (TSB)**

A platform from which to explore the broad range of publications in Translation and Interpreting (T&I) including transfer and mediation aspects of intra- and interlingual translation, intercultural communication, adaptation, interpreting, localization, multimedia translation, language mediation, terminology and documentation [Translation studies bibliography (TSB) 2019].

6.1.5 Selected Key Journals

- **Annual review of applied linguistics**

ISSN 0267-1905

ARAL provides cutting-edge and timely articles on a wide number of areas, including language learning and pedagogy, second language acquisition, sociolinguistics, language policy and planning, language assessment, and research design and methodology (Annual review of applied linguistics 2019).

- **Journal of second language writing**

ISSN 1060-3743

The Journal of Second Language Writing is a peer-reviewed academic journal in the fields of linguistics and language education. Its scope encompasses all aspects of second and foreign language writing, including writing instruction and assessment (Journal of second language writing 2018).

- **Applied linguistics**

ISSN 0142-6001

Applied Linguistics is a peer-reviewed academic journal in the field of applied linguistics established in 1980 and published by Oxford University Press (Applied linguistics 2019).

- **Studies in second language acquisition**

ISSN 0272-2631

Studies in Second Language Acquisition is a refereed journal of international scope devoted to the scientific discussion of acquisition or use of non-native and heritage languages (Studies in second language acquisition 2018).

- **Translation and interpreting studies**

ISSN 1932-2798

Translation and Interpreting Studies (TIS) is a peer-reviewed journal designed to disseminate knowledge and research relevant to all areas of language mediation (Translation and interpreting studies 2019).

- **Language and literature**

ISSN 0963-9470

Language and Literature is an invaluable international peer-reviewed journal that covers the latest research in stylistics, defined as the study of style in literary and non-literary language (Language and literature 2019).

- **Modern Chinese literature and culture**

ISSN 1520-9857

Modern Chinese Literature and Culture, formerly Modern Chinese Literature (1984–1998), is a peer-reviewed, scholarly journal devoted to the culture of modern and contemporary China, with "China" understood not in the narrow, political sense (Modern Chinese literature and culture 2019).

- **American Historical review**

ISSN 0002-8762

AHR has been the journal of record for the historical profession in the United States since 1895—the only journal that brings together scholarship from every major field of historical study (American Historical review 2019).

- **Journal of American history**

ISSN 0021-8723

The Journal of American History is the leading scholarly publication and journal of record in the field of American history and is the major resource for the study, investigation, and teaching of our country's heritage (Journal of American history 2019).

6.1.6 Translation Tools and Resources

- **Elsevier Web Shop—Translation Services**

Language translation services by experts who take care of translating your paper or presentation from or into Chinese, Portuguese, Spanish, Arabic, Turkish, Russian, German, Italian, Japanese, Korean and many more languages (Elsevier Web Shop —Translation Services 2019).

- **WorldLingo Free Translation Online**

Offers: Free (500 words) … text, document, website, or Email translations … as well as identifying the language in the Free Text option (WorldLingo Free Translation Online 2018).

- **Google Translate**

Google's free service instantly translates words, phrases, and web pages between English and over 100 other languages (Google Translate 2019).

- **Google Translated Search**

Find and read translated results from webpages in a foreign language.
GTS Translation Services—Free online translation tool
"Select the source and target languages, input the text and click Translate."
more … (Google Translate 2019).

- **Language Realm**

Free translation resources in English, Spanish, French, German, Latin, Chinese, and Japanese (Google Translate (Language Realm 2014).

- **TOMEDES Translation Conferences**

Searchable list of upcoming translation conferences (TOMEDES About Us 2019).

- **oTranscribe**

A free web app to assist with transcribing recorded interviews. Gives the user the ability to control speed and pace from keyboard. Keeps recordings privately on one's own hard drive (oTranscribe 2019).

6.2 Business and Management

6.2.1 Reference Books

	Title: Encyclopedia of management Location: 1/F A2 Reference Collection Status: LIB USE ONLY Call No. HD 30.15 Enc 2012 ISBN: 9781414459042 Ed. 7th Published: Farmington Hills, MI: Gale, Cengage Learning Year: c2012
	Title: Encyclopedia of business and finance (Electronic Resource) ISBN: 9780028662688 Ed. 3rd Publication Info: Farmington Hills, Mich.: Macmillan Reference USA, a part of Gale, Cengage Learning Year: 2014

(continued)

(continued)

	Title: The growing business handbook: inspiration and advice from successful entrepreneurs and fast growing UK companies/consultant editor, Adam Jolly (Electronic Resource) ISBN: 9780749470388 Ed. 15th Publication Info: London: Kogan Page Year: 2014
	Title: The global business handbook: the eight dimensions of international management/edited by David J. Newlands and Mark J. Hooper Location: 4/F A1 Business Administration Call No. HD 62.4 Glo 2009 ISBN: 9780566087479 Published: Farnham, England; Burlington, VT: Gower Publishing Year: c2009

6.2.2 *Featured Course Related Books*

	Title/Author: Intermediate Accounting: IFRS Edition/ Donald E. Kieso, Jerry J. Weygandt, Terry D. Wartield Call No. HF 5636 Wey 2018 ISBN: 9781119373001/9781119372936 Ed. 3rd Publisher: Wiley Year: 2018
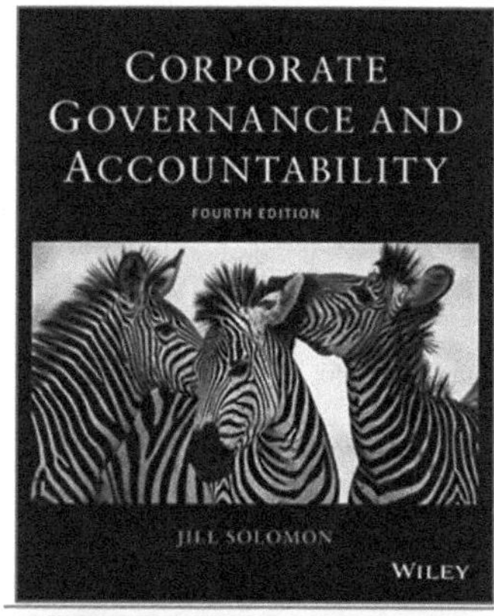	Title/Author: Corporate governance and accountability/ Jill Solomon Call No. HD 2741 Sol 2013 ISBN: 9781118449103 Ed. 4th Publisher: John Wiley and Sons Year: 2013
	Title/Author: The law and practice of Macau taxation/ Carlos Noronha Call No. KM3 4460 Nor 2012 Course code: ACCT442/ACCT4010 Name of Lecturer: Prof. Carlos Noronha ISBN: 9789882243743 Ed. 4th Publisher: Pearson Education Asia Year: 2012

(continued)

(continued)

	Title/Author: Financial accounting/Walter T. Hamison Jr., Baylor University, Charles T. Homgren, Stanford University, C. William (Bill) Thomas, Baylor University, Wendy M. Tietz, Kent State University Call No. HF 5636 Har 2017 ISBN: 9780134127620 Ed. 11th Publisher: Pearson Year: 2017
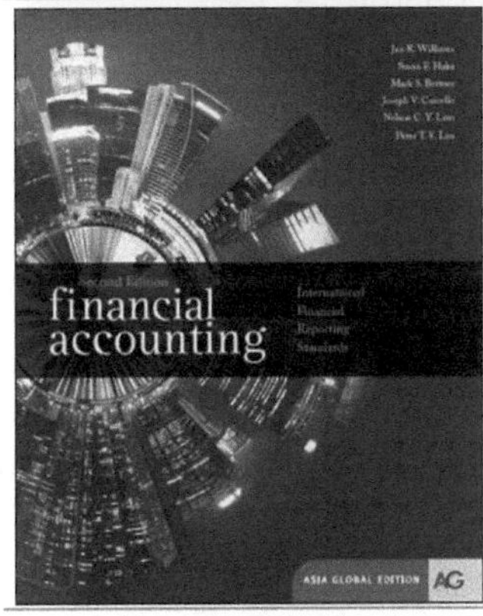	Title/Author: Financial accounting: international financial reporting standards/Jan R. Williams … [et al.] Call No. HF 5635 Fin 2015 ISBN: 9781259073625 Ed. 2nd Publisher: McGraw-Hill Year: 2012
	Title/Author: Principles of corporate finance/Richard A. Brealey, Stewart C. Myers, Franklin Allen Call No. HG 4026 Bre 2017 ISBN: 9781259253331 Ed. 12th Publisher: McGraw-Hill Education Year: 2017

(continued)

(continued)

	Title/Author: Cost management: a strategic emphasis/ Edward J. Blocher, David E. Stout, Paul E. Juras, Gary Cokins Call No. HF 5686 C8 Blo 2015 ISBN: 9780077733773 Ed. 7th Publisher: McGraw-Hill/Irwin Year: 2015
	Title/Author: Contemporary issues in accounting/ Michaela Rankin … [et al.] Call No. HF 5625 Con 2012 ISBN: 9780730300267/9780730300298 Ed. 1st Publisher: Wiley Year: 2012
	Title/Author: Modern database management/Jeff A. Hoffer, V. Ramesh, Heikki Topi Call No. QA 76.9 D3 Hof 2016 ISBN: 9781292101859 Ed. 12th Global Publisher: Pearson Year: 2016

(continued)

(continued)

	Title/Author: Social research methods: qualitative and quantitative approaches/W. Lawrence Neuman Call No. HM 571 Neu 2014 ISBN: 9781292020235 Ed. 7th Publisher: Pearson Education Year: 2014
	Title/Author: The micro economy today/Bradley R. Schiller, Karen Gebhardt Call No. HB 172 Sch 2019 ISBN: 9781260098532 Ed. 15th Publisher: McGraw-Hill Education Year: 2019
	Title/Author: Econometrics by example/Damodar Gujarati Call No. HB 139 Guj 2015 ISBN: 9781137375018 Ed. 2nd Publisher: Palgrave Year: 2015

(continued)

(continued)

 	Title/Author: International economics: theory end policy/Paul R. Krugman, Maurice Obstfeld, Marc J. Melitz Call No. HF 1359 Kru 2015 ISBN: 978292019550/9780133423648 Ed. 10th Global Publisher: Pearson Year: 2015
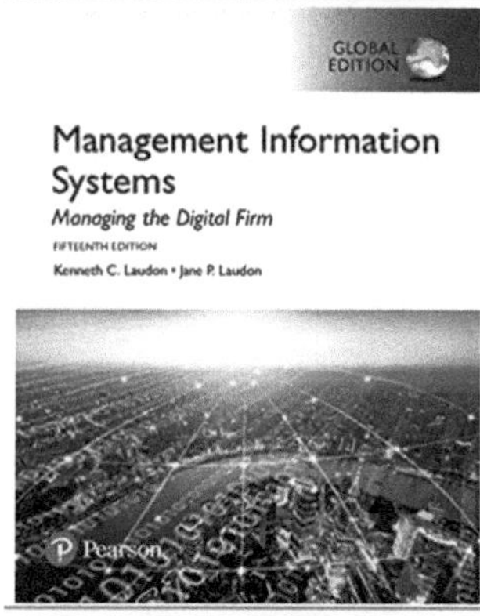 	Title/Author: Management information systems: managing the digital firm/Kenneth C. Laudon, Jane P. Laudon Call No. T 58.6 Lau 2018 ISBN: 9781292211756 Ed. 15th Global Publisher: Pearson Education Year: 2018
 	Title/Author: Fundamentals of corporate finance/ Jonathan Berk, Peter DeMarzo, Jarrad Harford Call No. HG 4026 Ber 2015 ISBN: 9781292068145 Ed. 3rd Publisher: Pearson Year: 2015

(continued)

(continued)

	Title/Author: Fundamentals of corporate finance (Revised edition)/Richard A. Brealey, London Business School, Stewart C. Myers, Sloan School of Management, Massachusetts Institute of Technology, Alan J. Marcus, Carroll School of Management, Boston College Call No. HG 4026 Bre 2018 ISBN: 9781259921964 Ed. 9th Publisher: McGraw-Hill Education Year: 2018
	Title/Author: Fundamentals of futures and options markets/John C. Hull Call No. HG 6024 A3 Hul 2017 ISBN: 9781292155036 Ed. 8th Global Publisher: Pearson Education Year: 2017
	Title/Author: Investments/Zvi Bodie [and three others] Call No. HG 4521 Bod 2014 ISBN: 9780071262286 Ed. Asia Global edition Publisher: McGraw-Hill Education Asia Year: 2014

(continued)

(continued)

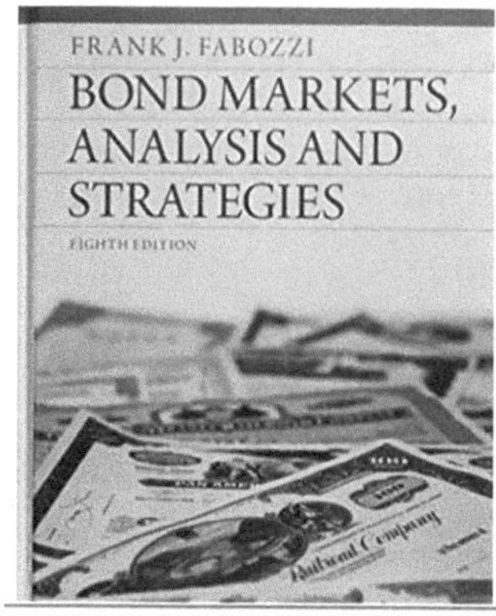	Title/Author: Bond markets, analysis, and strategies/ Frank J. Fabozzi Call No. HG 4651 Fab 2013 ISBN: 9780273766131/9780132743549 Ed. 8th Publisher: Pearson Year: 2013
	Title/Author: International financial management/Cheol S. Eun, Georgia institute of Technology, Bruce G. Resnick, Wake Forest University Call No. HG 3881 Eun 2018 Course code: FINC431/FINC4008 Name of Lecturer: Dr. Anna Vong ISBN: 9781259922190 Ed. 8th Publisher: McGraw-Hill Education Year: 2018
	Title/Author: Financial modeling/Simon Benninga; with a section on Visual Basic for applications by Benjamin Czaczkes Call No. HG 173 Ben 2014 ISBN: 9780262027281 Ed. 4th Global Publisher: The MIT Press Year: 2014

(continued)

(continued)

Title/Author: Financial risk manager handbook plus test bank: FRM Part I/Part II/Philippe Jorion
Call No. HD 61 Jor 2011
ISBN: 9780470904015
Ed. 6th
Publisher: John Wiley & Sons
Year: 2011

Title/Author: Corporate finance: core principles & applications/Stephe A. ROSS, Sloan School of Management, Massachusetts Institute of Technology, Randolph W. Westerfield, Marshall School of Business, University of Southern California, Jeffrey F. Jaffe, WhartOrtn School of Business, UniverSity of Pennsylvania, Bradford D. Jordan, Gatton College of Business and Economics, University of kentucky
Call No. HG 4026 Ros 2018
ISBN: 9781260083279/9781259289903
Ed. 5th
Publisher: McGraw-Hill Education
Year: 2018

Title/Author: Service quality management in hospitality, tourism, and leisure/edited by Jay Kandampully, Connie Mok, Beverley Sparks
Call No. 2010 TX 911.3 M27 Ser
ISBN: 9780789011411
Ed. 1st
Publisher: Routledge Taylor & Francis
Year: 2010

(continued)

(continued)

	Title/Author: Human resources management in the hospitality industry/David K. Hayes, Jack D. Ninemeier Call No. TX 911.3 P4 Hay 2016 ISBN: 9781119030867/9781118988503 Ed. 2nd Publisher: Wiley Year: 2016
	Title/Author: The interpersonal communication book/ Joseph A. DeVito Call No. BF 637 C45 DeV 2016 ISBN: 9781292099996 Ed. 14th Global Publisher: Pearson Year: 2016
	Title/Author: International business: the challenges of globalization/John J. Wild, Kenneth L. Wind Call No. HD 62.4 Wil 2016 ISBN: 9781292095042 Ed. 8th Publisher: Pearson Education Limited Year: 2016

(continued)

(continued)

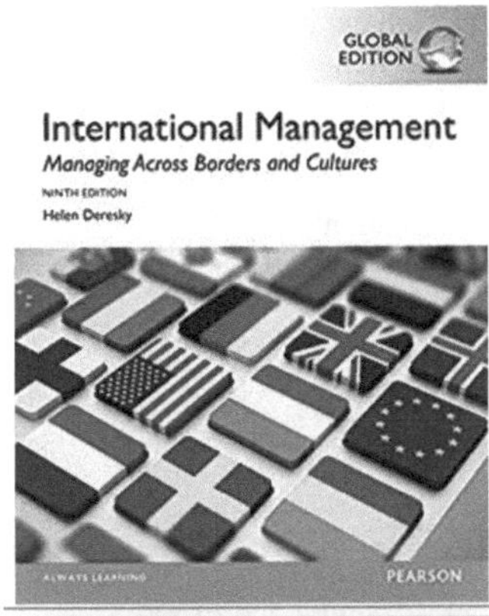	Title/Author: International management: managing across borders and cultures: text and cases/Helen Deresky, Professor Emerita, State University of New York-Plattsburgh Call No. HD 62.4 Der 2017 ISBN: 9781292153537/9780134376042 Ed. 9th Global Publisher: Pearson Year: 2017
	Title/Author: Asian business & management: theory, practice and perspectives/edited by Harukiyo Hasegawa, Carlos Noronha Call No. HD 70 A78 Asi 2009 ISBN: 9780230545069 Ed. 1st Publisher: Palgrave Macmillan Year: 2009
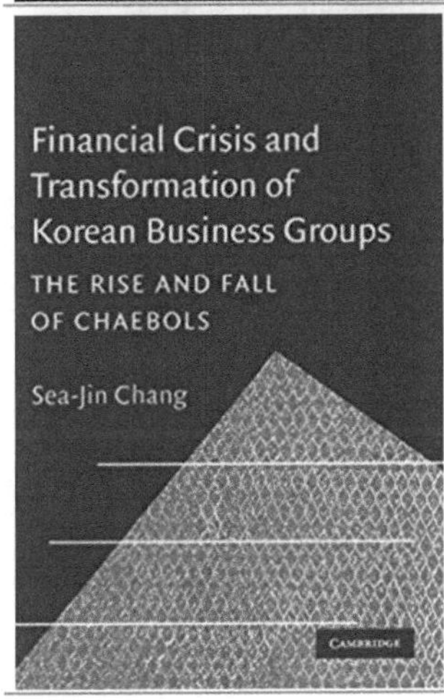	Title/Author: Financial crisis and transformation of Korean business groups: the rise and fall of chaebols/Sea Jin Chang Call No. HG 4247 Cha ISBN: 0521814359 Ed. 1st Publisher: Cambridge University Press Year: 2003

(continued)

(continued)

	Title/Author: Intercultural communication in contexts/ Judith N. Martin, Thomas K. Nakayama Call No. HM 1211 Mar 2018 ISBN: 9781259251795/9780073523934 Ed. 7th Publisher: McGraw-Hill Education Year: 2018
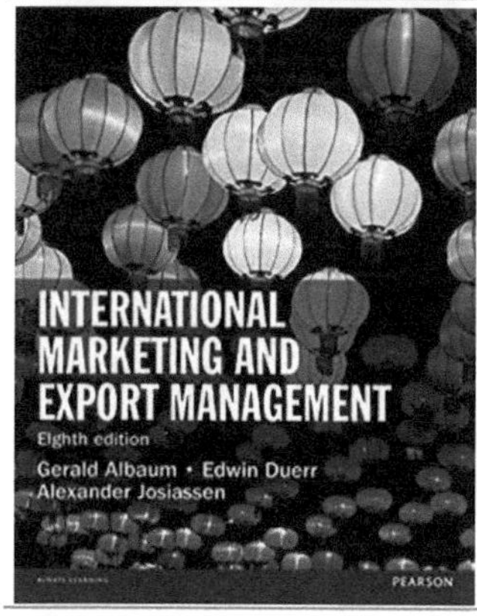	Title/Author: International marketing and export management/Gerald Albaum, University of New Mexico, USA, Edwin Duerr, San Francisco State University, USA, Alexander Josiassen Copenhagen Business School, Denmark Call No. HF 1416 A16 2016 ISBN: 9781292016924 Ed. 8th Publisher: Pearson Year: 2016
	Title/Author: Introductory mathematical analysis for business, economics, and the life and social sciences/E. Haeussler, R. Paul, R. Wood Call No. QA 300 Hae 2014 ISBN: 9781292021140 Ed. 13th new international Publisher: Pearson Education Year: 2014

(continued)

(continued)

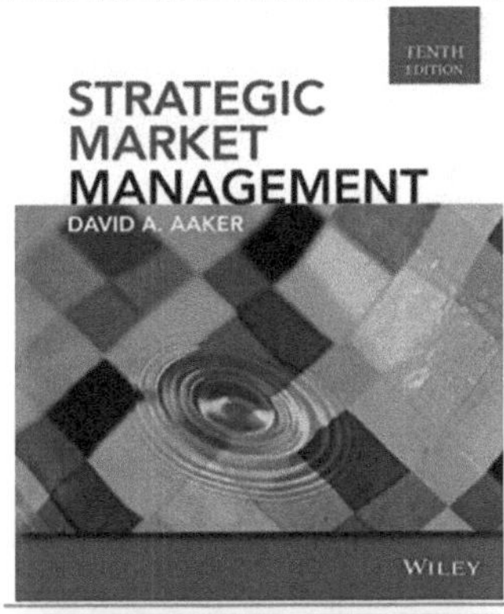	Title/Author: Strategic market management/David A. Aaker, Vice Chairman, Prophet Professor Emeritus, University of California, at Berkeley Call No. HF 5415.13 Aak 2014 ISBN: 9781118582862 Ed. 10th Publisher: John Wiley & Sons Year: 2014
	Title/Author: Business statistic: a first course/David M. Levine Call No. HF 1017 Lev 2016 ISBN: 9781292095936 Ed. 7th Global Publisher: Pearson Year: 2016
	Title/Author: Statistics For managers using Microsoft Excel/David M. Levine, David F. Stephan, Kathryn A. Szabat Call No. HD 30.215 Lev 2017 ISBN: 9781292156347 Ed. 8th Global Publisher: Pearson Education Limited Year: 2016

(continued)

(continued)

	Title/Author: Management/Stephen P. Bobbins, Mary Coulter Call No. HD 31 Rob 2018 ISBN: 9781292215839 Ed. 14th Publisher: Pearson Education Year: 2018
	Title/Author: MGMT220 business communication/ instructor, Yuko Matsumolo, Gordon Kerr, Joanne Chan Call No. HF 5718 Mat 2016 ISBN: 9781308862545 Ed. 1st Publisher: McGraw Hill Education Year: 2016
	Title/Author: Essentials of marketing research/Babin and Armstrong Call No. HF 5415.2 Bab 2016 ISBN: 9781305263475 Ed. 6th Publisher: Cengage Year: 2016

(continued)

(continued)

	Title/Author: Research methods for business: a skill-building approach/Uma Sekaran and Roger Bougie Call No. HD 30.4 Sek 2016 ISBN: 9781119165552 Ed. 7th Publisher: John Wiley & Sons Year: 2016
	Title/Author: Performance management/Herman Aguinis Call No. HF 5549.5 R3 Agu 2013 ISBN: 9781292024073/9780132556385 Ed. 3rd Publisher: Pearson Year: 2013
	Title/Author: Strategic compensation: a human resource management approach/Joseph J. Martocchio Call No. HF 5549.5 C67 Mar 2015 ISBN: 9780133457100/9781292058863 Ed. 8th Publisher: Pearson Education Limited Year: 2015

(continued)

(continued)

	Title/Author: Contemporary strategy analysis/Robert M. Grant Call No. HD 30.28 Gra 2016 ISBN: 9781119120834 Ed. 9th Publisher: John Wiley Year: 2016
	Title/Author: Principles of marketing/Philip Kotler, Gary Armstrong with Mare Oliver Opresnik Call No. HF 5415 Kot 2018 ISBN: 9781292220178 Ed. 17th Global Publisher: Pearson Education Year: 2018
	Title/Author: International marketing/Philip R. Cateora, Mary C. Gilly, John L. Graham, R. Bruce Money Call No. HF 1416 Cat 2016 ISBN: 9781259253065 Ed. 17th Publisher: McGraw-Hill Education Year: 2016

(continued)

(continued)

	Title/Author: Leisure marketing: a global perspective/ Susan Horner and John Swarbrooke Call No. GV 188 Hor 2005 ISBN: 9780750655507 Publisher: Elsevier/Butterworth Heinemann Year: 2005
	Title/Author: Marketing management/Philip Kotler, Kevin Lane Keller Call No. HF 5415.13 Kot 2016 ISBN: 9780133856460 Ed. 15th Publisher: Pearson Education Year: 2016
	Title/Author: Project management: a managerial approach/Jack R. Meredith, Samuel J. Mantel, Jr. (deceased), Scott M. Shafer Call No. HD 69 P75 Mer 2016 ISBN: 9781118945834 Ed. 9th Asia Global Publisher: John Wiley & Sons Year: 2016

6.2.3 *Academic Writing and Citation Resources*

APA style is an author-date citation style which was developed for use in psychology but has been widely-adopted by other disciplines including business, management, economics and education.

There are two major components to the APA author-date style

- the in-text author-date citation at the appropriate place within the text of the document, e.g. (Smith 2010), and
- the detailed reference list at the end of the document.

Instructions and examples can be found in the following books.

	Title: Academic writing for international students of business/Stephen Bailey Location: 2/F C3 Language & Literature Call No. PN 151 Bai 2011 ISBN: 9780415564700 Published: London: Routledge Year: 2011
	Title: Academic writing: writing and reading in the disciplines/Janet Giltrow Location: 2/F C3 Language & Literature Call No. PE 1408 Gil 2002 ISBN: 1551113953 Ed. 3rd Published: Peterborough, Ont.; Orchard Park, NY: Broadview Press Year: 2002

(continued)

(continued)

	Title: Academic writing [electronic resource]: a guide for management students and researchers/Mathukutty M. Monippally and Badrinarayan Shankar Pawar ISBN: 9788132104414 Published: Los Angeles: Response Year: 2010
	Title: Publication manual of the American Psychological Association Location: 1/F A2 Reference Collection Call No. BF 76.7 Pub 2010 ISBN: 9781433805592 Published: Washington, DC: American Psychological Association Year: c2010

6.2.4 Key Databases

- **ABI/INFORM Global**

The ABI/INFORM Collection contains ABI/INFORM Global™ is one of the most comprehensive business databases on the market, offering the latest business and financial information for researchers at all levels. It includes in-depth coverage from thousands of publications, most of them in full-text. With ABI/INFORM Global, users can find out about business conditions, management techniques, business trends, management practice and theory, corporate strategy and tactics, and competitive landscape. ABI/INFORM Global includes ABI/INFORM Archive, which offers a deep backfile of many of the most important business journals of the last century (ABI/INFORM Global 2019).

- **Business Plan Handbook Collection**

Here you can find examples of how to approach, structure and compose business plans. Examples are taken from businesses in the manufacturing, retail and service industries (Business Plan Handbook 2019).

- **Business Source Complete**

Business Source Complete is an upgraded version of Business Source Premier and replaces ABI/Inform. It is the world's definitive scholarly business database, providing the ultimate collection of bibliographic and full text content. As part of the comprehensive coverage offered by this database, indexing and abstracts for the most important scholarly business journals back to 1886 are included. In addition to the searchable cited references, Business Source Complete contains detailed author profiles for the most-cited authors in the database. Journal ranking studies reveal that Business Source Complete is the overwhelmingly superior database for full text journals in all disciplines of business, including marketing, management, MIS, POM, accounting, finance and economics. Additional full text, non-journal content includes financial data, books, monographs, major reference works, book digests, conference proceedings, case studies, investment research reports, industry reports, market research reports, country reports, company profiles, SWOT analyses and more (Business Source Complete 2019).

- **CEIC Data**

CEIC provides access to over 5 million macro-economic time series and statistics from more than 190 countries and contains databases such as Global Database, China Premium Database, and World Trend Plus. China Premium Database is, in particular, a leading economic time-series database, focused exclusively on the Chinese market that contains historical data dating back to 1949. Use when you need international economic, industrial and financial trends data. Times-series can be directly retrieved from the database and imported into Excel (About 2019).

- **Accounting and Tax**

ProQuest Accounting and Tax Database provides centralized access to top journals, reference reports, proceedings, dissertations and more, including over 2,300 publications with hundreds in full-text.

ProQuest Accounting and Tax includes:

- Highly ranked global and scholarly journals, including all journals from the American Accounting Association
- Accounting, tax management, and auditing trade publications from top publishers such as CCH, Aspen, Thompson Professional and Regulatory Services, Source Media, Tax Management Inc., and Euromoney
- AICPA publications
- Tax law and financial law publications from notable sources such as the American Bar Association and American Law Institute
- Global accounting and tax journals from the UK, Canada, Australia, France, Spain, Ireland and more
- Financial advising, governance, and risk management publications from Incisive Media, CFA Institute, and Association for Financial Counseling and Planning
- Over 1,500 accounting dissertations
- More than 7,800 Working Papers from SSRN (Social Science Research Network)
- Select conference proceedings for accounting (Accounting et al. 2019).

- **Government Finance Statistics (GFS)**

The Government Finance Statistics (GFS) contains data for all reporting countries in the framework of the Government Finance Statistics Manual, 2014(GFSM 2014. The GFSM 2014 classifications remain largely the same as in the GFSM 2001 presentations. GFS data are compiled either on a cash basis of recording or non-cash basis of recording (e.g., an accrual basis or a commitment basis). GFS contains detailed data on revenue, expense, transactions in assets and liabilities, and stocks positions in assets and liabilities of general government and its subsectors. GFS also includes preset presentations of GFS data by country, and by indicator, and also provides the option to download data with customized queries (Government Finance Statistics (GFS) 2018).

- **International Financial Statistics (IFS)**

The International Financial Statistics database covers about 200 countries and areas, with some aggregates calculated for selected regions, plus some world totals. Topics covered include balance of payments, commodity prices, exchange rates, fund position, government finance, industrial production, interest rates, international investment position, international liquidity, international transactions, labor statistics, money and banking, national accounts, population, prices, and real effective exchange rates (Government Finance Statistics (International Financial Statistics (IFS) 2016) 2018).

- **ProQuest Asian Business and Reference**

ProQuest Asian business and reference offers detailed information on companies, economies, markets, and overall business conditions throughout the Eastern Hemisphere. A great deal of information on international trade is available as well. It contains: news and current awareness sources, country information and statistics, information on people and institutions, and on policy and analysis (Asian & European Business Collection 2019).

- **Wind 資訊 (金融終端及經濟數據終端)**

> Wind 資訊經濟終端專注于證券經紀業務市場，全面滿足分析師對客戶進行專業化服務的 ... 報告、市場傳聞等即時資訊，第一時間獲悉機構持倉、盈利預測等關鍵資料的動態變化。 ... 全球金融市場綜合屏(0)、股指期貨綜合屏 (6)，提供全球最重要市場最重要品種的全面即時行情。 ... 新基金和基金日曆，綜合基金發行、分紅等公告及資料。

(Wind 資訊 (金融終端及經濟數據終端) 2011).

6.2.5 Selected Key Journals

- **Quarterly journal of economics**

ISSN 0033-5533

The Quarterly Journal of Economics (QJE) is the oldest professional journal of economics in the English language. It covers all aspects of the field—from the journal's traditional emphasis on microtheory, to both empirical and theoretical macroeconomics (Quarterly journal of economics 2019).

- **Journal of Human Resources**

ISSN 0022-166X

The Journal of Human Resources is among the leading journals in empirical microeconomics. Intended for scholars, policy makers, and practitioners, each issue examines research in a variety of fields, including labor economics, development economics, health economics, and the economics of education, discrimination, and retirement (Journal of Human Resources 2019).

- **Academy of Management Review**

ISSN 0363-7425

The Academy of Management Review is a peer-reviewed academic journal on management (Academy of Management Review 2017).

- **Journal of Management**

ISSN 0149-2063

Journal of Management (JOM) peer-reviewed and published bi-monthly, is committed to publishing scholarly empirical and theoretical research articles that have a high impact on the management field as a whole. JOM covers domains such as business strategy and policy, entrepreneurship, human resource management, organizational behavior, organizational theory, and research methods (Journal of Management 2019).

- **Journal of the academy of marketing science**

ISSN 0092-0703

The Journal of the Academy of Marketing Science (JAMS) is devoted to the study and improvement of marketing and serves as a vital link between scholarly research and practice by publishing research-based articles in the substantive domain of marketing (Journal of the academy of marketing science 2019).

- **Journal of Marketing**

ISSN 0022-2429

The Journal of Marketing (JM) develops and disseminates knowledge about real-world marketing questions relevant to scholars, educators, managers, consumers, policy makers and other societal stakeholders. It is the premier outlet for substantive research in marketing (Journal of Marketing 2019).

- **Journal of service research**

ISSN 1094-6705

Journal of Service Research (JSR), peer-reviewed and published quarterly, is widely considered the world's leading service research journal. It is a must read to keep up with the latest in service research. Practical and readable, JSR offers the necessary knowledge and tools to cope with an increasingly service-based economy. JSR features articles by the world's leading service experts, from both academia and the business world (Journal of service research 2019).

6.2.6 Macao Business and Management Resources

- **Monetary Authority of Macao (澳門金融管理局)**

Including history and responsibilities, banking, other licensees authorized investment funds, insurance, statistics, rules and guidelines, Macao currency in circulation and other statistics in Macau publicity and sales (Monetary Authority of Macao 2019).

- **Statistics and Census Service, Macau (澳門統計暨普查局)**

Statistics and Census Service (DSEC) is to provide timely and comprehensive information on the latest development of Macao. DSEC conducts more than 60 statistical projects every year, covering various demographic, social and economic aspects. Data collected from the surveys, after processing and analysis, are aggregated to statistical indicators, tables and graphs, which are disseminated on the DSEC website, in press release, publication, etc (Service and Products 2017).

- **Macao's External Merchandise Trade Statistics Database (澳門對外商品貿易統計資料庫)**

Macao's External Merchandise Trade Statistics Database established by Government of Macao Special Administrative Region Statistics and Census Service. It includes Macau goods and trading partners' statistics (Macao's External Merchandise Trade Statistics Database 2017).

- **Financial Statements of Macau Limited Companies (澳門股份有限公司財務報表)**

The Financial Statements of Macau Limited Companies is a self-built database of the University of Macau Library, which is used to query the financial statements of the major 148 commercial establishments in Macau (Financial Statements of Macau Limited Companies 2014).

6.3 Education

6.3.1 Reference Books

	Title: 中國教育大百科全書 = The Chinese encyclopedia of education/ 主編顧明遠 Location: 1/F A2 Reference Collection Call No. LA 1131.82 Chu 2012 v.1(~v.5) ISBN: 9787544445672 Published: 上海市: 上海教育出版社 Year: 2012
	Title: International encyclopedia of education/ editors-in-chief, Penelope Peterson, Eva Baker, Barry McGaw Location: 1/F A2 Reference Collection Call No. LB 15 Int 2010 v.1(~v.8) ISBN: 9780080448930 Ed. 3rd Published: Oxford: Academic Press Year: c2010

(continued)

(continued)

	Title: Handbook of research on curriculum reform initiatives in English education/ Christopher Denman and Rahma Al-Mahrooqi, editors (Electronic Resources) ISBN: 9781522558477 Published: Hershey, Pennsylvania (701 E. Chocolate Avenue, Hershey, Pennsylvania, 17033, USA): IGI Global Year: 2019
	Title: Handbook of research on E-assessment in higher education/Ana Azevedo and Jose Azevedo, editors ISBN: 9781522559375 Published: Hershey, Pennsylvania (701 E. Chocolate Avenue, Hershey, Pennsylvania, 17033, USA): IGI Global Year: 2019

(continued)

(continued)

	Title: Higher Education: Handbook of Theory and Research [electronic resource]: Published under the Sponsorship of the Association for Institutional Research (AIR) and the Association for the Study of Higher Education (ASHE)/edited by Michael B. Paulsen ISBN: 9783319724904 Published: Cham: Springer International Publishing: Imprint: Springer Year: 2018

6.3.2 Featured Course Related Books

	Title/Author: Foundations of education/Allan C. Ornstein … [et al.] Call No. LB 17 Fou 2014 ISBN: 9781133589853 Ed. 12th Publisher: Wadsworth Cengage Learning Year: 2014

(continued)

(continued)

	Title/Author: Foundations of education/Allan C. Omstein, Daniel U. Levine Call No. LB 17 Orn 2008 ISBN: 9780618904129 Ed. 10th Publisher: Cengage Learning Year: 2008
	Title/Author: Children and their development/ Robert V. Kail Call No. HQ 767.9 Kai 2015 ISBN: 9780133595680 Ed. 7th Publisher: Pearson Education Year: 2015
	Title/Author: Very young learners/Vanessa Reilly & Sheila M. Ward Call No. PE 1128 A2 Rei 1997 ISBN: 9780194372091 Ed. 1st Publisher: Oxford University Press Year: 1997 This book includes activities with practical ideas and advice for teaching English to very young students.

(continued)

(continued)

	Title/Author: Educational psychology/Anita Woolfolk Call No. LB 1051 Hoy 2016 ISBN: 9781292095301 Ed. 13th Publisher: Pearson Education Year: 2016
	Title/Author: What should every EFL teacher know?/Paul Nation Call No. PE 1128 A2 Nat 2013 ISBN: 9781599662664 Ed. 1st Publisher: Compass Publishing Year: 2013

(continued)

(continued)

<table>
<tr>
<td>
</td>
<td>Title/Author: Educational administration: concepts and practices/Fred C. Lunenburg, Allan C. Ornstein
Call No. LB 2805 Lun 2012
ISBN: 9781111353971
Ed. 6th
Publisher: Cengage Learning
Year: 2012</td>
</tr>
<tr>
<td>
</td>
<td>Title/Author: 教育管理學:概念與實踐/ Fred C. Lunenburg, Allan C. Ornstein 著;朱志勇，鄭磊主譯
Call No. LB 2805 Lun 2013
ISBN: 9787501989522
Ed. 1版
Publisher: 中國輕工業出版社
Year: 2013</td>
</tr>
</table>

(continued)

(continued)

	Title/Author: Ways of seeing (Chinese edition) 觀看之道/John Berger 約翰.伯格 Call No. N 7430.5 Ber 2015 Course code: GELH2005 Name of Lecturer: Ms. Fanny, Shuk Fan Wong ISBN: 9787549558575 Publisher: Guangxi Normal University Press 廣西師範大學出版社 Year: 2015
	Title/Author: Understanding art history from famous paintings (Chinese edition) 從名畫瞭解藝術史/Zhang Xinlong 張心龍 Call No. N 5300 Cha 2011 ISBN: 9787308085038 Publisher: Zhejiang University Press 浙江大學出版社 Year: 2011
	Title/Author: 幼兒社會教材教法/作者: Carol, Seefeldt, Sharon Castle and Renee C. Falconer; 譯者:蕭美華，謝瑩慧，吳雅玲 Call No. LB 1530 See 2010 ISBN: 978986654497 Ed. 2 版 Publisher: 華騰文化 Year: 2010

6.3.3 Academic Writing and Citation Resources

Research in education is typically cited in APA style. Use selected resources for academic writing and citation at Sect. 6.2.3 as your references.

6.3.4 Key Databases

- **Educator Reference Collection**

Perfect for educating future teachers and administrators, these references cover the latest technologies, developments, instruction and coaching breakthroughs as well as background information on child health and development (Educator Reference Collection 2018).

- **ERIC**

The Education Resources Information Center is an online digital library of education research and information, it is sponsored by the Institute of Education Sciences of the United States Department of Education, contains more than 2,200 digests along with references for additional information and citations and abstracts from over 1,000 educational and education-related journals (Education Resources Information Center 2018).

- **ProQuest career and technical education**

ProQuest Career and Technical Education is the definitive source for vocational information. The database includes over 600 titles, with more than 500 available in full text. Both students and instructors can access the database to research virtually any technical topic, including:

Computing science, Healthcare, Building trades, Auto mechanics, Sales and retail, Accounting, Graphic design, Photography.

Agricultural Research, Computer Technology Review, Law and Order, Nutrition and Food Science, and Printed Circuit Design are just a few of the titles available in ProQuest Career and Technical Education (Career and Technical Education Database 2019).

- **ProQuest education journals**

Education Database supports the study and application of education across all levels of education, including early childhood education, primary and secondary education, and higher education. The database supports global study and research, including thousands of full-text journals, dissertations and other relevant sources (Education database 2019).

- **The Hong Kong education bibliographic database**

It aims at offering an easy-to-use one-stop search platform that covers all research works on education in Hong Kong. At present, it consists of over 10,000 bibliographic citations of research works, including books and book chapters, articles from periodicals, dissertations or theses, conference papers, research reports and other relevant materials, covering research dating back as far as 1946 (The Hong Kong Education Bibliographic Database 2014).

6.3.5 Selected Key Journals

- **Review of educational research**

ISSN 0034-6543

Review of Educational Research (RER) publishes critical, integrative reviews of research literature bearing on education. Such reviews should include conceptualizations, interpretations, and syntheses of literature and scholarly work in a field (Review of education research 2018).

- **Internet and higher education**

ISSN 1096-7516

The Internet and Higher Education, a is quarterly journal devoted to addressing contemporary issues and future developments related to online learning, teaching, and administration on the Internet in post-secondary settings. It is a peer-reviewed journal intended to be a vehicle for scholarly presentation (Internet and higher education 2019).

- **Educational Research Review**

ISSN 1747-938X

Educational Research Review is an international journal addressed to researchers and various agencies interested in the review of studies and theoretical papers in education at any level. The journal accepts high quality articles that are solving educational research problems by using a review approach (Educational Research Review 2019).

- **Computers and education**

ISSN 0360-1315

Computers and Education aims to increase knowledge and understanding of ways in which digital technology can enhance education, through the publication of high quality research, which extends theory and practice (Computers and education 2019).

- **Educational psychologist**

ISSN 0046-1520

The Educational Psychologist is a quarterly peer-reviewed academic journal published by Routledge on behalf of Division 15 (Educational Psychology) of the American Psychological Association. The journal publishes conceptual and review articles rather than empirical studies on all aspects of educational psychology (Educational psychologist 2018).

- **Educational Researcher**

ISSN 0013-189X

Educational Researcher (ER) contains scholarly articles of general significance to the educational research community from a wide range of disciplines. focusing on manuscripts that examine the significance of research in education and developments important to the field of educational research (Educational Researcher 2019).

- **Learning and instruction**

ISSN 0959-4752

As an international, multi-disciplinary, peer-refereed journal, Learning and Instruction provides a platform for the publication of the most advanced scientific research in the areas of learning, development, instruction and teaching (Learning and instruction 2019).

- **The Modern Language Journal**

ISSN 0026-7902

A refereed publication, The Modern Language Journal is dedicated to promoting scholarly exchange among teachers and researchers of all modern foreign languages and publishes documented essays, quantitative and qualitative research studies, response articles, and editorials that challenge paradigms of language learning and teaching (The Modern Language Journal 2019).

- **Language teaching**

ISSN 0261-4448

Language Teaching is the essential research resource for language professionals providing a rich and expert overview of research in the field of second-language teaching and learning (Language teaching 2017).

- **Early childhood research quarterly**

ISSN 0885-2006

Early Childhood Research Quarterly (ECRQ) publishes research on early childhood education and development from birth through 8 years of age and predominantly empirical research (quantitative or qualitative methods) on issues of interest to early childhood development, theory, and educational practice (Early childhood research quarterly 2019).

- **Topics in early childhood special education**

ISSN 0271-1214

Topics in Early Childhood Special Education is a peer-reviewed academic journal that publishes papers in the field of Education (Topics in early childhood special education 2019).

6.4 Law

6.4.1 Reference Books

	Title: The philosophy of law. Volume 2, K-Z [electronic resource]: an encyclopedia/editor, Christopher Berry Gray ISBN: 0203800222 Published: New York: Garland Pub. Year: 1999
	Title: Encyclopedia of public international law/ published under the auspices of the Max Planck Institute for Comparative Public Law and International Law; under the direction of Rudolf Bernhardt Location: 1/F A2 Reference Collection Status: LIB USE ONLY Call No. KZ 1160 Enc v.1 (~v.5) ISBN: 0444862447 Published: Amsterdam: North-Holland Year: 1992–2000

(continued)

(continued)

	Title: 國際比較法百科全書. 第 1 卷, 各國法律制度概況 / [捷]維克托 . 納普主編;高紹先,夏登峻 ... [等]譯. Location: 4/F C1 Law & Public Administration Call No. K 48 Int 2002 v.1 c.2 ISBN: 750363586X Published: 北京市:法律出版社 Year: 2002
	Title: West's encyclopedia of American law [electronic resource]/Jeffrey Lehman, Shirelle Phelps, project editors ISBN: 0787693731 Ed. 2nd Published: Detroit, Mich.: Thomson Gale Year: c2005

(continued)

(continued)

	Title: The Max Planck encyclopedia of European private law/edited by Jurgen Basedow, Klaus J. Hopt, Reinhard Zimmermann, with Andreas Stier Location: 4/F C1 Law & Public Administration Call No. K 3824.1 M3 Max 2012 v.1 (~v.2) ISBN: 9780199578955 Published: Oxford: Oxford University Press Year: 2012

6.4.2 *Featured Course Related Books*

	Title/Author: The BRICS-lawyers' guide to global cooperation/edited by Rostam J. Neuwirth, Alexandr Svetlicinii, Denis De Castro Halis Call No. K 3823 BRI 2017 ISBN: 9781108416238 Ed. 1st Publisher: Cambridge University Press Year: 2017

6.4.3 *Citing and Referencing*

The Faculty of Law of the University of Macau publishes works in Chinese, this summary introduces GB/T 7714-2005 rules for the bibliography of information and literature.

Chinese Standard GB/T 7714-2005 was developed mainly for use in publishing Chinese articles in various disciplines.

The following examples demonstrate the format for some commonly used of electronic and print sources.

Book
[1] Rowling J. K. Harry Potter and the Philosopher for some com 第1版. London: Bloomsbury Publishing Inc, 1997.

Journal
[2] Petit C, Sieffermann J. Testing consumer preferences for iced-coffee: Does the drinking environment have any influence? [J]. Food Quality and Preference, 2007, 18(1): 161–172.

Website
[3] Tran M. Barack Obama To Be America's First Black President [EB/OL]. The Guardian (2008-11-05) [2019-02-22]. https://www.theguardian.com/world/2008/nov/05/uselections20083.

Podcast
[4] THIS AMERICAN LIFE. 640: Five Women [J]. WBEZ Radio, 2018.

You are highly suggested to refer to "ISO 690:2010, Information and documentation—Guidelines for bibliographic references and citations to information resources, NEQ" for the detailed way to identify all sources.

6.4.4 *Key Databases*

- **Criminal justice reference collection**

It offers online collection on periodicals and reference information for legal study. It offers online collection on periodicals and reference information for legal study (Criminal justice reference collection 2019).

- **HeinOnline**

HeinOnline is a research database for legal literature, providing full text access to legal journals and other legal materials from seven collections, namely, Law Journal Library, Federal Register Library, Treaties and Agreements Library, U.S. Supreme

Court Library, European Center for Minority Issues, U.S. Attorney General Opinions and Legal Classics (HeinOnline 2014).

- **Hong Kong Legal Information Institute**

The Hong Kong Legal Information Institute (HKLII—pronounced 'H K Lee') is a free access legal information system developed and jointly operated by the University of Hong Kong Department of Computer Science and Faculty of Law, with the kind assistance of the Australasian Legal Information Institute (AustLII). The system is based on data obtained from sources in Hong Kong and the region. Mark-up, processing, database structure, search engine facilities, and some other aspects of technical infrastructure are adapted from software provided by AustLII. The Hong Kong, China and Taiwan pages (and some subject pages) of the World Law index are jointly prepared by HKU Faculty of Law and AustLII [Hong Kong Legal Information Institute (HKLII) 2014].

- **Lexis**

This source is particularly useful for those in law as it includes comprehensive legal materials, such as cases, statutes, and law reviews. It also offers some of the most authoritative and some exclusive collections of news, business, legal and public records data (Lexis.com 2014).

- **Parry and Grand encyclopaedic dictionary of international law**

It includes increased coverage in growing areas of international law including diplomatic law, criminal law, human rights, and more. Entries provides the reader with copious references for further research including cases, treaties, journal articles, and websites (Parry and Grant Encyclopaedic Dictionary of International Law 2014).

- **ProQuest criminal justice**

Criminal Justice Database is a comprehensive database supporting research on crime, its causes and impacts, legal and social implications, as well as litigation and crime trends. As well as U.S. and international scholarly journals, it includes correctional and law enforcement trade publications, dissertations, crime reports, crime blogs and other material relevant for researchers or those preparing for careers in criminal justice, law enforcement and related fields (ProQuest criminal justice 2019).

- **The making of modern law: foreign, comparative, and international law**

The Making of Modern Law: Foreign, Comparative and International Law, 1600–1926, gives any library the kind of historical resources previously found only at the largest and oldest repositories and gives even the most extensive libraries online access to foreign and international legal literature. FCIL includes pre-1926 treatises and similar monographs, sourced from the collections of the Yale, George Washington University, and Columbia law libraries, in the following areas: International Law; Comparative Law; Foreign Law; Roman Law; Islamic Law; Jewish Law; and Ancient Law (The making of modern law: foreign, comparative, and international law 2012).

- **Westlaw China**

Westlaw China is a searchable database of source documents related to international trade law and launched by Thomson Reuters. It offers full text reports for WTO and other international organizations. It is updated daily to ensure the most current and accurate information (Westlaw China 2019).

- **WorldTradeLaw**

WorldTradeLaw.net offers both a free resource library of current trade news and resources, as well as a subscription service (the DSC Service), which provides summary and analysis of all WTO reports and arbitrations; a current keyword index; a database of dispute settlement tables and statistics; and a user-friendly search tool for WTO cases, legal texts, and other documents (WorldTradeLaw 2019).

- **北大法意**

北京法意科技有限公司成立於2003年1月，是引領中國法律資訊化的知名企業。公司主營業務聚焦法律應用軟體發展和法律資料智慧應用兩大領域。公司部分產品已經在法院、教育行業全系統應用，具有全國影響力。本數據庫為法學研究與案例教學的中文法律資訊數據庫(北大法意 2019).

- **北大法寶**

北大法寶 1985 年誕生於北大法律系，是由北大英華公司和北京大學法制資訊中心共同開發和維護的法律 資料庫產品，經過 20 多年的不斷創新，目前已發展成為法律法規、司法案例、法學期刊、律所實務、專題參考、英文譯本、法寶視頻和司法考試八大檢索系統，在內容和功能上保持領先，已成為法律資訊服務領導品牌，是法律工作者的必備工具，受到國內外客戶的一致好評。同時，基於北大法寶龐大內容支援的法律軟體發展業務日益受到用戶青睞
(北大法寶 2018).

- **法源法律網**

本數據庫內容涵蓋台灣的法規類別、判解函釋、裁判書、法學論著索引等單元，並提供最新法律新聞、法規新訊、判解新訊、函釋新訊、法規草案及法律論著等各項資料
(法源法律網 2014).

- **萬律**

萬律(Westlaw China) 中國法律法規雙語資料庫是湯森路透法律資訊集團基於世界領先的 Westlaw 法律資訊平臺的技術和經驗，為中國和英語世界的中國法律執業人士提供智慧的法律資訊檢索、全面的法律知識及中國法律研究解決方案
(萬律 2019).

6.4.5 Selected Key Journals

- **Yale law journal**

ISSN 0044-0094

The Yale Law Journal is a student-run law review affiliated with the Yale Law School. Published continuously since 1891, it is the most widely known of the eight law reviews published by students at Yale Law School. The journal is one of the most cited legal publications in the nation and usually generates the highest number of citations per published article (The Yale Law Journal 2019).

- **Stanford law review**

ISSN 0038-9765

The Stanford Law Review (SLR) is a legal journal produced independently by Stanford Law School students (Stanford law review 2018).

- **Harvard law review**

ISSN 0017-811X

The Harvard Law Review is a student-run organization whose primary purpose is to publish a journal of legal scholarship (Harvard law review 2019).

- **Common market law review**

ISSN 0165-0750

The Common Market Law Review is a bi-monthly, peer-reviewed law journal covering European Union law (Common Market Law Review 2018).

- **European journal of psychology applied to legal context**

ISSN 1889-1861

This journal is aimed at researchers, academics and professionals in Psychology, Law, Social Work, Forensic Sciences, Educators and, in general, people related with Social Sciences and the Law (European journal of psychology applied to legal context 2019).

- **American journal of international law**

ISSN 0002-9300

AJIL is a leading peer-reviewed journal, published quarterly since 1907. It features articles, essays, editorial comments, current developments, and book reviews by pre-eminent scholars and practitioners from around the world addressing developments in public and private international law and foreign relations law (American journal of international law 2016).

- **Chinese journal of international law**

ISSN 1540-1650

The Chinese Journal of International Law is a quarterly peer-reviewed law journal covering international law. Since 2005 it is published by Oxford University Press in association with the Chinese Society of International Law and the Institute of International Law (Wuhan University) (Chinese journal of international law 2017).

- **Psychology crime and law**

ISSN 1068-316X

Psychology, Crime and Law is a peer-reviewed academic journal covering forensic psychology (Psychology crime and law 2018).

- **Journal of legal analysis**

ISSN 2161-7201

The Journal of Legal Analysis, founded in 2009, is a fully open access peer-reviewed general journal on all aspects of law, centered at Harvard Law School but with a board of editors drawn from many universities (Journal of legal analysis 2019).

- **Law probability and risk**

ISSN 1470-8396

Law, Probability and Risk is a fully refereed journal which publishes papers dealing with topics on the interface of law and probabilistic reasoning (Law probability and risk 2019).

- **Journal of legal studies**

ISSN 0047-2530

Journal of Legal Studies (JLS) publishes interdisciplinary academic research about law and legal institutions. It emphasizes social science approaches, especially those of economics, political science, and psychology (Journal of legal studies 2018).

6.4.6 Resources for Macau Legal Studies

- **Legis Mac (澳門法例資料查詢系統)**

Legis Mac, while maintaining the original issues of the Macau Official Gazette, the law No. descriptive word, enact Year, effective conditions for access points, now also highlights the simplified query methods and increases Chinese stroke query function (LegisMac 2014).

- **Macau Government Printing Bureau (澳門印務局)**

This includes government bodies and organs of the notice and announcement, public institutions, societies and Macau regulations (Macau Government Printing Bureau 2019).

- **Publications of Macao Special Administrative Region Legislative Assembly**

The Legislative Assembly of the Macao Special Administrative Region is the legislature of the region. Its publications are mostly published in three forms: compilation, legal book and journal, and its contents are legally authoritative (Publications of Macao Special Administrative Region Legislative Assembly 2017).

- **The Centre for Law Studies publications**

The Centre for Law Studies of the Faculty of Law, University of Macau has published a Collection of Law textbooks and the Bulletins of the Faculty of Law, which serve to prepare the juridical bibliography and to create public awareness of the Macao Law (The Centre for Law Studies publications 2018).

6.5 Social Science

6.5.1 Reference Books

	Title: The international encyclopedia of communication [electronic resource]/edited by Wolfgang Donsbach ISBN: 9781405131995 Published: Malden, MA: Blackwell Pub. Year: 2008
	Title: The Sage encyclopedia of social science research methods/edited by Michael S. Lewis-Beck, Alan E. Bryman, Tim Futing Liao Location: 1/F A2 Reference Collection Status: LIB USE ONLY Call No. H 62 Sag v.1 (~v.3) ISBN: 0761923632 Published: Thousand Oaks, CA: Sage Year: c2004
	Title: Sociology of work: an encyclopedia/edited by Vicki Smith Location: 1/F A2 Reference Collection Status: LIB USE ONLY Call No. HD 6955 Soc 2013 v.1 (~v.2) ISBN: 9781452205069 Published: Thousand Oaks, CA: SAGE Reference Year: 2013

(continued)

(continued)

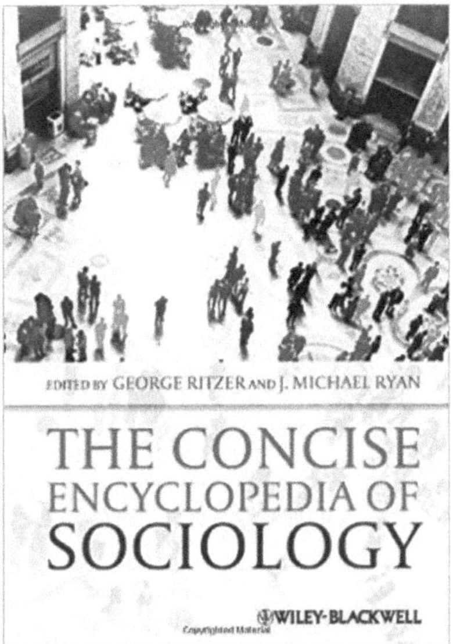	Title: The concise encyclopedia of sociology/ edited by George Ritzer and J. Michael Ryan Location: 1/F A2 Reference Collection Call No. HM 425 Con 2011 ISBN: 9781405183536 Published: Chichester, West Sussex, U.K.: Wiley-Blackwell Year: 2011
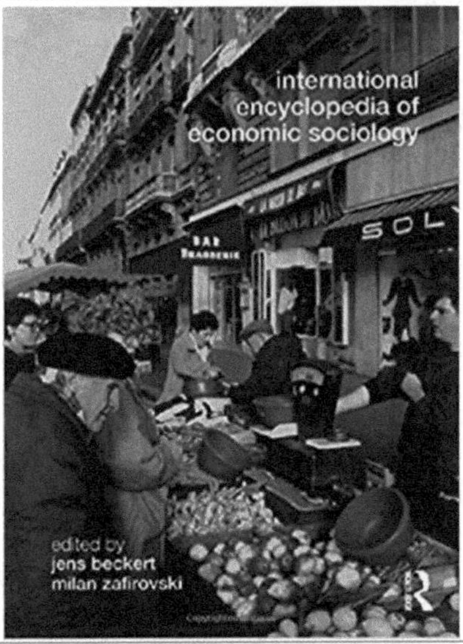	Title: International encyclopedia of economic sociology [electronic resource]/edited by Jens Beckert, Milan Zafirovski ISBN: 9780415286732 Published: Abingdon, Oxon; New York: Routledge Year: c2011

(continued)

(continued)

	Title: Encyclopedia of sociology [electronic resource]/Edgar F. Borgatta, editor in chief; Rhonda J. V. Montgomery, managing editor ISBN: 002865899X Published: New York, N.Y.: Macmillan Reference USA Year: c2000
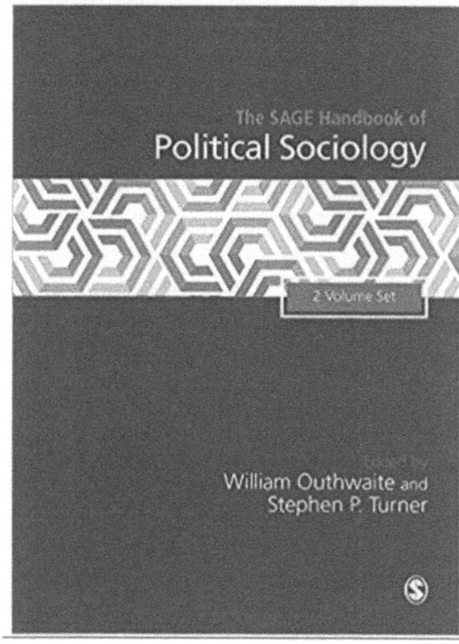	Title: The Sage handbook of political sociology/ edited by William Outhwaite and Stephen P. Turner ISBN: 9781526416483 Published: Los Angeles; London; Thousand Oaks, California: Sage Year: 2018

(continued)

(continued)

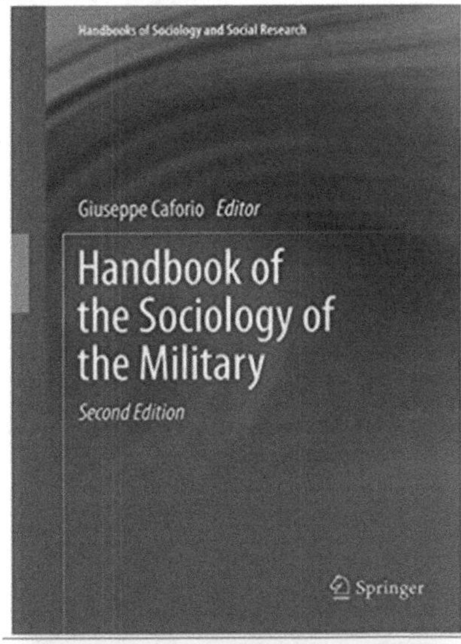	Title: Handbook of the Sociology of the Military [electronic resource]/edited by Giuseppe Caforio, Marina Nuciari ISBN: 9783319716022 Published: Cham: Springer International Publishing: Imprint: Springer Year: 2018
	Title: A handbook for social science field research: essays & bibliographic sources on research design and methods/edited by Ellen Perecman, Sara R. Curran Location: 4/F A1 Business Administration Call No. H 62 Han 2006 ISBN: 1412916801 Published: Thousand Oaks, CA: Sage Publications Year: c2006

(continued)

(continued)

	Title: A handbook of social science research/ Gary D. Bouma, G. B. J. Atkinson Location: 4/F A1 Business Administration Call No. H 62 Bou 1995 ISBN: 0198280009 Published: Oxford; New York: Oxford University Press Year: 1995
	Title: Comparative world data: a statistical handbook for social science/Georg P. Muller with the collaboration of Volker Bornschier Location: 1/F A2 Reference Collection Call No. HA155 MUL ISBN: 0801837340 Published: Baltimore: Johns Hopkins University Press Year: c1988

6.5.2 Featured Course Related Books

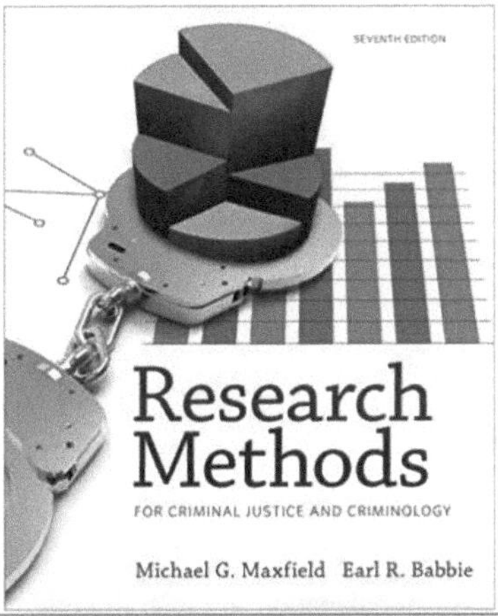	Title/Author: Research methods for criminal justice and criminology/Michael G. Maxfield, Earl R. Babbie Call No. HV 7419.5 Max 2015 Publisher: Cengage Learning Year: 2015
	Title/Author: Crime prevention/Nick Tilley Call No. HV 7431 Til 2012 ISBN: 9781317821779/9781843923947 Ed. 1st Publisher: Taylor & Francis Year: 2014

(continued)

(continued)

	Title/Author: Handbook of Crime Prevention and Community Safety/Nick Tilley Call No. HV 7431 Han 2017 ISBN: 9781317821779/9781843923947 Ed. 2nd Publisher: Routledge Year: 2017
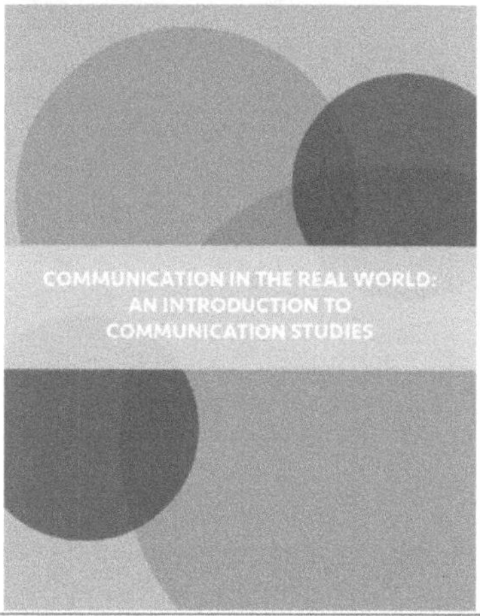	Title/Author: Communication in the real world: an introduction to communication studies [electronic resource] ISBN: 9781946135070 Publisher: University of Minnesota Libraries Publishing Year: 2019

(continued)

(continued)

	Title/Author: Public relations: strategies and tactics/Dennis L. Wilcox, School of Journalism & Mass Communications, San Jose State University, Glen T. Cameron, School of Journalism, University of Missouri, Bryan H. Reber, Grady College of Journalism & Mass Communications, University of Georgia Call No. HM 1221 Wil 2015 ISBN: 9781292056586/9780205960644 Ed. 11th Publisher: Pearson Year: 2015
	Title/Author: Essentials of understanding psychology/Robert S. Feldman, University of Massachusetts Amherst Call No. BF 121 Fel 2017 ISBN: 9781259531804/9781259253423 Ed. 12th Publisher: McGraw-Hill Education Year: 2017

(continued)

(continued)

	Title/Author: Beginning university: thinking, researching and writing for success/Andrew Wallace, Tony Schirato & Philippa Bright Call No. LB 2395 Wal 1999 ISBN: 9781864488890 Ed. 1st Publisher: Allen & Unwin Year: 1999
	Title/Author: Lifespan development/Denise Boyd, Helen Bee Call No. BF 713 Boy 2015 ISBN: 0133815854/9780133805666 Ed. 7th Publisher: Pearson Education Year: 2015

(continued)

(continued)

	Title/Author: Social psychology/David G. Myers Call No. HM 1033 Mye 2017 ISBN: 9780077861971/9781259251139 Ed. 12th Publisher: McGraw-Hill Year: 2017 Connecting Social Psychology to the world around us.
	Title/Author: Intimate relationships/Rowland S. Miller, Sam Houston State University Call No. HQ 10 Mil 2015 ISBN: 9780077861803 Publisher: McGraw-Hill Year: 2015

(continued)

(continued)

	Title/Author: Personality psychology/Daniel Cervone, Lawrence A. Pervin Call No. BF 698 Cer 2014 ISBN: 9781118322215 Ed. 12th ed, International student version Publisher: John Wiley & sons Singapore Pte. Ltd. Year: 2014
	Title/Author: Sociology of deviant behavior/ Marshall B. Clinard, Emeritus, University of Wisconsin, Robert F. Meier University of Nebraska at Omaha Call No. HM 811 Cli 2016 ISBN: 9781133594154 Publisher: Cengage Learning Year: 2016

(continued)

(continued)

<table>
<tr>
<td>
</td>
<td>Title/Author: The sociology of gambling in China/T. J. Cheng
Call No. HV 6722 C5 Che 2011
ISBN: 9781844640805
Ed. 1st
Publisher: Social Sciences Academic Press
Year: 2011</td>
</tr>
<tr>
<td>
</td>
<td>Title/Author: Chopsticks and gambling/ Desmond Lam
Call No. HV 6722 CS Lam 2014
ISBN: 9781412853934
Ed. 1st
Publisher: Routledge
Year: 2017</td>
</tr>
</table>

(continued)

(continued)

	Title/Author: Profit without honor: white-collar crime and the looting of America/Stephen M. Rosoff, Henry N. Pontell, Robert Tillman Call No. HV 6769 Ros 2014 ISBN: 9780133008500 Ed. 6th Publisher: Pearson Education Year: 2014

6.5.3 Academic Writing and Citation Resources

Research in education is typically cited in APA style. Use selected resources for academic writing and citation at Sect. 6.2.3 for further information.

6.5.4 Key Databases

- **Communication and Mass Media Complete**

Communication and Mass Media Complete provides a good-quality research database in areas related to communication and mass media. This database originated with the acquisition and subsequent merging of two popular databases in the fields of communication and mass media studies. There were CommSearch [formerly produced by the National Communication Association (NCA)], and Mass Media Articles Index (formerly produced by Pennsylvania State University) (Communication and Mass Media Complete 2019).

- **Communication Abstract**

Communication Abstracts is a bibliographic database for communication and mass media studies. It provides cover-to-cover indexing and abstracts for hundreds of top journals covering communication and other closely-related fields of study (Communication Abstract 2019).

- **The Times Digital Archive**

The Times Digital Archive is an online, full-text facsimile of more than 200 years of the Times, one of the most highly regarded resources for eighteenth-, nineteenth-, and twentieth-century news coverage, with every page of every issue from 1785 to 2013. This historical newspaper archive allows researchers an unparalleled opportunity to search and view the best-known and most cited newspaper in the world online in its original published context (The Times Digital Archive 2014).

- **香港影評庫**

為推廣本地影評文化，保存香港影評人多年來的文字成果，香港電影評論學會特設立「香港影評庫」，目標是蒐集影評人歷年的影評文章，進行有系統的分類存檔。

(香港影評庫 2019).

- **Gale Primary Sources**

Gale Primary Sources allows researchers to uncover primary source documents in archives. Gale Primary Sources includes Associated Press Collections Online, Brazilian and Portuguese History and Culture, Nineteenth Century Collections Online, The Economist Historical Archive, 1843–2011, The Financial Times Historical Archive, 1888–2010, The Illustrated London News Historical Archive, 1842–2003, The Making of Modern Law: Legal Treatises, 1800–1926, The Sunday Times Digital Archive, 1822–2006 and The Times Digital Archive (Gale Primary Sources 2019).

- **Brazilian and Portuguese History and Culture**

This collection turns the spotlight on South America's largest and most influential power, covering topics such as: colonialism, missionaries, slave trade and abolition, economic development and agricultural trade, Indigenous Peoples, international relations, and the fight for Brazilian independence (Brazilian et al. 2019).

- **East India Company**

East India Company offers access to a unique collection of India Office Records from the British Library, London. Containing royal charters, correspondence, trading diaries, minutes of council meetings and reports of expeditions, among other document types, this resource charts the history of British trade and rule in the Indian subcontinent and beyond from 1600 to 1947 (East India Company 2017).

- **Nineteenth Century Collection Online**

The Nineteenth Century Collections Online advisory board was formed with two integral goals in mind: to furnish scholars with the best, most diverse content and to offer users a cutting-edge platform designed to support online research. The advisory board's role is to suggest topics, themes, concepts, and regions of study, and to recommend the institutions, associations, and scholars needed to provide expert input and identify specific collections (Political, Economic, and Military Conditions in China: Reports and Correspondence of the U.S 2011).

- **Political, Economic, and Military Conditions in China: Reports and Correspondence of the U.S.**

It reproduces the six principal MID files relating exclusively to China for the period 1918 to 1941 (general conditions, political conditions, economic conditions, army, navy, and aeronautics). Also includes documents created by other U.S. Government agencies and foreign governments from the records of the Military Intelligence Division (Political, Economic, and Military Conditions in China 2014).

- **Military** and **Government Collection**

This database designed to offer current news pertaining to all branches of the military and government, offers a thorough collection of periodicals, academic journals, and other content pertinent to the increasing needs of those sites. It provides cover-to-cover full text for nearly 300 journals and periodicals and indexing and abstracts for nearly 400 titles (Military and Government Collection 2014).

- **ProQuest Military Collection**

The Military Database covers topics across all government and military branches, including international relations, political science, criminology, defense, aeronautics and space flight, communications, civil engineering, and more. An important benefit of the Military Database is its content diversity. Included are scholarly journals, trade and industry journals, magazines, technical reports, conference proceedings, government publications, and more (ProQuest Military Collection 2014).

- **ProQuest Political Science**

ProQuest Political Science covers the literature of political science and international relations, including such topics as comparative politics, political economy, international development, environmental policy, and hundreds of related topics (ProQuest Political Science 2019).

- **ProQuest Social Science Journals**

Social Science Database offers indexing and full text for hundreds of academic journals, providing extensive coverage across a wide range of social science disciplines including anthropology, communication, criminology, economics, education, political science, psychology, social work, and sociology (ProQuest Social Science Journals 2019).

- **PsycArticles**

PsycARTICLES is a definitive source of searchable full-text, peer-reviewed scholarly and scientific articles in psychology. The database contains more than 40,000 articles from 56 journals—45 published by the American Psychological Association (APA) and 11 from allied organizations. It includes all journal articles, letters to the editor and errata from each journal. Coverage spans 1985 to present (PsycARTICLES 2019).

- **PsycBooks**

PsycBOOKS is an extensive collection of peer-reviewed books that provides students, researchers, and educators access to high-quality publications in psychology and related fields.

PsycBOOKS includes the newest scholarly and professional books published by APA including reference works from the APA Handbooks in Psychology® Series that delve deep into specific subfields within psychology (PsycBooks 2019).

- **PsycInfo**

PsycINFO, from the American Psychological Association (APA), contains more than 2 million citations and summaries of scholarly journal articles, book chapters, books, and dissertations, all in psychology and related disciplines, dating as far back as the 1800s. Ninety-seven percent of the covered material is peer-reviewed. Journal coverage, which spans 1887 to present, includes international material selected from nearly 2,000 periodicals in more than 25 languages (PsycInfo 2014).

6.5.5 *Selected Key Journals*

- **Journal of communication**

ISSN 0021-9916

The Journal of Communication is a bimonthly peer-reviewed academic journal that publishes articles and book reviews on a broad range of issues in communication theory and research (Journal of communication 2019).

- **Communication research**

ISSN 0093-6502

Communication Research (CR), peer-reviewed and published bi-monthly, has provided researchers and practitioners with the most up-to-date, comprehensive and important research on communication and its related fields (Communication research 2019).

- **New media and society**

ISSN 1461-4448

New Media and Society engages in critical discussions of the key issues arising from the scale and speed of new media development, drawing on a wide range of disciplinary perspectives and on both theoretical and empirical research (New media and society 2019).

- **Personality and social psychology review**

ISSN 1088-8683

Personality and Social Psychology Review is an official journal of SPSP, the Society for Personality and Social Psychology, Inc. It is the premiere outlet for original theoretical papers and conceptual review articles in all areas of personality and social psychology (Personality and social psychology review 2019).

- **Social issues and policy review**

ISSN 1751-2395

Social Issues and Policy Review (SIPR) provides state of the art and timely theoretical and empirical reviews of topics and programs of research that are directly relevant to understanding and addressing social issues and public policy (Social issues and policy review 2019).

- **European review of social psychology**

ISSN 1046-3283

The European Review of Social Psychology (ERSP) is an international open-submission review journal, published under the auspices of the European Association of Social Psychology (European review of social psychology 2019).

- **Public administration review**

ISSN 0033-3352

Public Administration Review is a bimonthly peer-reviewed academic journal covering research, theory, and practice in the field of public administration (Public administration review 2019).

- **Journal of public administration research and theory**

ISSN 1053-1858

The Journal of Public Administration Research and Theory was established in the late 1980s to serve as a bridge between public administration and public management scholarship on the one hand, and public policy studies on the other (Journal of public administration research and theory 2019).

- **Annual review of sociology**

ISSN 0360-0572

The Annual Review of Sociology, in publication since 1975, covers the significant developments in the field of Sociology. Topics covered in the journal include major theoretical and methodological developments as well as current research in the major subfields (Annual review of sociology 2019).

- **Sociological methods and research**

ISSN 0049-1241

Sociological Methods and Research is a quarterly journal devoted to sociology as a cumulative empirical science. The scope is broad and flexible, and authors are invited to correspond with the editors about the appropriateness of their articles (Sociological methods and research 2019).

6.5.6 *Resources for Macau Studies*

- **Virtual Library of Macau (澳門虛擬圖書館)**

Virtual Library of Macau provides a full-text library of information about Macao, Macao scholar's information and academic trends in Maca., Macau Foundation published books and journals full text (You can create your own account Login to obtain the full text).

The virtual library project will focus on academic research in Macau, which can be roughly divided into three parts:

- **Macau Full Library**

  1. Upload the hundreds of books and periodicals published by the Macao Foundation on the Internet
  2. Contact relevant institutions and authors to obtain authorization to access the Internet for books published by other institutions and upload them to the Internet.

- **Macau Scholar Information**
  Upload the introduction of Macau scholars and related academic papers on the Internet for the reference of those who study Macau.
- **Academic Trends in Macau**
  Sort out and categorize recent academic activities held in Macau for people who have interests in knowing the recent academic development in Macao (Virtual Library of Macau 2018).

- **Global mapping of Macau (全球地圖中的澳門)**
  The project of Global Mapping of Macao is organized by Macau University of Science and Technology (MUST) and sponsored by Macao Foundation, running by the Institute for Social and Cultural Research (ISCR) and the University Library. This project is in pursuit of development of a special collection of old maps about Macao. These are gathered from all over the world by collecting or facsimileing. According to the license of the provenance of the maps, the permitted maps are the digitized and presented in this non-commercial database, which is open access for the global scholars and Macao citizens. There are eight topics of the database: City Plans of Macao, Macao and its surroundings, Macao in Routes, Images of Macao, Macao in China Maps, Macao in East Indies Maps, Macao in Asia Maps, and Macao in World Maps (Global mapping of Macau 2018).

- **UM Macau Studies Databases (澳門大學澳門研究數據庫)**

UM Macau Studies Databases is a series of databases independently developed by the University of Macau library for Macao Studies. It includes:

- Ancient poetic cliff inscriptions in Macao (澳門古代摩崖石刻詩詞)
- Chinese Historical Journals of Guangdong-Hong Kong-Macao Full-text (粵港澳中文歷史期刊全文數據庫)
- Macau Conference Portal (澳門會議目錄及論文索引)
- Macau Fulltext Electronic Resources (澳門電子資源全文網)
- Macau Music Database (澳門音樂人資料庫)
- Macau Periodical Index (澳門期刊論文索引)
- UM Digital Museum Collection (澳大數位博物館館藏)
- UM Publications (澳大出版品)
- UM Videos Database (澳大視頻)
- Historical Archive of Va Kio Daily (澳門華僑報歷史檔案資料庫)
- The Va Kio Daily was published in Macao on November 20, 1937 and has a history of over 80 years. The Va Kio Daily records the development of Chinese society and the Macao region and is a precious historical document (Databases 2014)

References

ABI/INFORM Global (2019) Products. https://www.proquest.com/products-services/abi_inform_global.html. Accessed 08 Mar 2019

About CEIC (2019) Financial data & economic indicators. https://www.ceicdata.com/en/about-us. Accessed 08 Mar 2019

Academy of Management Review (2017) Wikipedia. https://en.wikipedia.org/wiki/Academy_of_Management_Review. Accessed 08 Mar 2019

Accounting, Tax and Banking Collection (2019) ProQuest. https://www.proquest.com/products-services/pq_accounting.html. Accessed 08 Mar 2019

America: History and Life (2019) EBSCO. https://www.ebsco.com/products/research-databases/america-history-and-life. Accessed 07 Mar 2019

American Historical review (2019) Oxford academic. https://academic.oup.com/ahr/pages/About. Accessed 08 Mar 2019

American journal of international law (2016) American Journal of International Law. https://ajil.scholasticahq.com/. Accessed 08 Mar 2019

Annual review of applied linguistics (2019) Annual Review of Applied Linguistics | Cambridge Core. https://www.cambridge.org/core/journals/annual-review-of-applied-linguistics. Accessed 07 Mar 2019

Annual review of sociology (2019) JSTOR: Annual Review of Sociology https://www.jstor.org/journal/annurevisoci?item_view=journal_info. Accessed 11 Mar 2019

Applied linguistics (2019) Applied Linguistics (journal)—Wikipedia. https://en.wikipedia.org/wiki/Applied_Linguistics_(journal). Accessed 07 Mar 2019

Art and humanities citation index (A&HCI) (2014) University of Macau—Wu Yee Sun Library. https://library.umac.mo/html/databases/e_databases_id_res.asp?getsuid=5. Accessed 07 Mar 2019

Asian & European Business Collection (2019) ProQuest. https://www.proquest.com/products-services/pq_asian_business.html. Accessed 08 Mar 2019

Books on China online University of Macau—Wu Yee Sun Library. https://library.umac.mo/html/databases/e_databases_id_res.asp?getsuid=6. Accessed 07 Mar 2019

Brazilian and Portuguese History and Culture (2019) The Oliveira Lima Library | FIU Libraries. https://libraries.fiu.edu/blog/ballm/trial-brazilian-portuguese-history-culture-oliveira-lima-library. Accessed 08 Mar 2019

Business Plan Handbook (2019) Advameg. https://www.referenceforbusiness.com/business-plans/. Accessed 08 Mar 2019

Business Source Complete (2019) EBSCO. https://www.ebsco.com/products/research-databases/business-source-complete. Accessed 08 Mar 2019

Career & Technical Education Database (2019) ProQuest. https://www.proquest.com/products-services/pq_career_tech_ed.html. Accessed 08 Mar 2019

China and Modern World (2014) University of Macau—Wu Yee Sun Library. https://library.umac.mo/html/databases/e_databases_id_res.asp?getsuid=6. Accessed 07 Mar 2019

China: Culture and Society (2014) The Wason pamphlet collection, Cornell University in SearchWorks catalog. https://searchworks.stanford.edu/view/12780043. Accessed 07 Mar 2019

Chinese journal of international law (2017) Wikipedia. https://en.wikipedia.org/wiki/Chinese_Journal_of_International_Law. Accessed 08 Mar 2019

Common Market Law Review (2018) Wikipedia. https://en.wikipedia.org/wiki/Common_Market_Law_Review. Accessed 08 Mar 2019

Communication Abstract (2019) EBSCO. https://www.ebsco.com/products/research-databases/communication-abstracts. Accessed 08 Mar 2019

Communication research (2019) SAGE Journals. https://journals.sagepub.com/home/crx. Accessed 11 Mar 2019

Communication and Mass Media Complete (2019) EBSCO. https://www.ebsco.com/products/research-databases/communication-mass-media-complete. Accessed 08 Mar 2019

Computers and education (2019) Journal—Elsevier. https://www.journals.elsevier.com/computers-and-education. Accessed 08 Mar 2019

Criminal justice reference collection (2019) Home Page. http://go.galegroup.com/ps/start.do?p=GVRL.mcricjr&u=macaucri. Accessed 08 Mar 2019

Early childhood research quarterly (2019) Journal—Elsevier. https://www.journals.elsevier.com/early-childhood-research-quarterly. Accessed 08 Mar 2019

Early English books online (2019) About early english books online—EEBO. https://eebo.chadwyck.com/about/about.htm. Accessed 07 Mar 2019

East India Company (2017) East India Company in SearchWorks catalog. https://searchworks.stanford.edu/view/12084840. Accessed 08 Mar 2019

Education database (2019) ProQuest. https://www.proquest.com/products-services/pq_ed_journals.html. Accessed 08 Mar 2019

Education Resources Information Center (2018) Wikipedia. https://en.wikipedia.org/wiki/Education_Resources_Information_Center. Accessed 08 Mar 2019

Educational psychologist (2018) Wikipedia. https://en.wikipedia.org/wiki/Educational_Psychologist_(journal). Accessed 08 Mar 2019

Educational Research Review (2019) Journal—Elsevier. https://www.journals.elsevier.com/educational-research-review. Accessed 08 Mar 2019

Educational Researcher (2019) SAGE Journals. https://journals.sagepub.com/home/edr. Accessed 08 Mar 2019

Educator Reference Collection (2018) University of Macau—Wu Yee Sun Library. https://library.umac.mo/html/databases/e_databases_title.asp?getid=E. Accessed 08 Mar 2019

Elsevier Web Shop—Translation Services (2019) Translation services for authors—services—Elseviers. https://www.journals.elsevier.com/phytomedicine/services/translation-services-for-authors. Accessed 08 Mar 2019

European journal of psychology applied to legal context (2019) The European Journal of Psychology Applied to Legal Context. https://journals.copmadrid.org/ejpalc/. Accessed 08 Mar 2019

European review of social psychology (2019) European Association of Social Psychology. https://www.easp.eu/publications/ersp/. Accessed 11 Mar 2019

Films on demand (2014) University of Macau—Wu Yee Sun Library. http://library.umac.mo/html/databases/e_databases.asp. Accessed 07 Mar 2019

Financial Statements of Macau Limited Companies (2014) UM digital library portal. http://libdigital.umac.mo/was5/digital/financial_report.jsp. Accessed 08 Mar 2019

Fonte Academica (2014) University of Macau—Wu Yee Sun Library. https://library.umac.mo/html/databases/e_databases_id_res.asp?getsuid=6. Accessed 07 Mar 2019

Fuente Academica (2014) University of Macau—Wu Yee Sun Library. https://library.umac.mo/html/databases/e_databases_id_res.asp?getsuid=6. Accessed 07 Mar 2019

Gale Primary Sources (2019) Home. https://www.gale.com/intl/primary-sources. Accessed 08 Mar 2019

Global mapping of Macau (2018) About. http://gmom.must.edu.mo/#aboutus. Accessed 11 Mar 2019

Google Translate (2019) Google translate. https://translate.google.com/. Accessed 08 Mar 2019

Google Translate (2019) Chrome web store. https://chrome.google.com/webstore/detail/google-translate/aapbdbdomjkkjkaonfhkkikfgjllcleb?hl=en. Accessed 08 Mar 2019

Government Finance Statistics (GFS) (2018) At a glance—IMF data. http://data.imf.org/?sk=a0867067-d23c-4ebc-ad23-d3b015045405. Accessed 08 Mar 2019

Harvard law review (2019) About the Harvard Law Review. https://harvardlawreview.org/about/. Accessed 08 Mar 2019

HeinOnline (2014) University of Macau—Wu Yee Sun Library https://library.umac.mo/html/databases/e_databases.asp. Accessed 08 Mar 2019

Historical reproduction (2014) University of Macau—Wu Yee Sun Library. http://library.umac.mo/html/databases/e_databases.asp. Accessed 07 Mar 2019

Hong Kong Legal Information Institute (HKLII) (2014) University of Macau—Wu Yee Sun Library https://library.umac.mo/html/databases/e_databases.asp. Accessed 08 Mar 2019

International Financial Statistics (IFS) (2016) At a glance—IMF data. https://data.imf.org/?sk=4C514D48-B6BA-49ED-8AB9-52B0C1A0179B. Accessed 08 Mar 2019

Internet and higher education(2019) Journal—Elsevier. https://www.journals.elsevier.com/the-internet-and-higher-education. Accessed 08 Mar 2019

Journal of the academy of marketing science (2019) Springer. https://link.springer.com/journal/11747. Accessed 08 Mar 2019

Journal of American history (2019) Oxford academic. https://academic.oup.com/jah/pages/About. Accessed 08 Mar 2019

Journal of communication (2019) Wikipedia. https://en.wikipedia.org/wiki/Journal_of_Communication. Accessed 11 Mar 2019

Journal of Human Resources (2019) UW Press journals—about the UW Press journals. http://jhr.uwpress.org/site/misc/about.xhtml. Accessed 08 Mar 2019

Journal of legal analysis (2019) Oxford Academic. https://academic.oup.com/jla. Accessed 08 Mar 2019

Journal of legal studies (2018) HeinOnline. https://home.heinonline.org/titles/Law-Journal-Library/Journal-of-Legal-Studies/?letter=J. Accessed 08 Mar 2019

Journal of Management (2019) Journal of management: SAGE journals. https://journals.sagepub.com/home/jom. Accessed 08 Mar 2019

Journal of Marketing (2019) SAGE Publications Ltd. https://uk.sagepub.com/en-gb/asi/journal-of-marketing/journal203561#description. Accessed 08 Mar 2019

Journal of public administration research and theory (2019)J-PART. https://www.jstor.org/journal/jpubladmiresethe?item_view=journal_info. Accessed 11 Mar 2019

Journal of second language writing (2018) Journal of Second Language Writing—Wikipedia. https://en.wikipedia.org/wiki/Journal_of_Second_Language_Writing. Accessed 07 Mar 2019

Journal of service research (2019) SAGE Journals. https://journals.sagepub.com/home/jsr. Accessed 08 Mar 2019

Military & Government Collection (2014) University of Macau—Wu Yee Sun Library. http://library.umac.mo/html/databases/e_databases.asp. Accessed 08 Mar 2019

New media and society (2019) SAGE Journals. https://journals.sagepub.com/home/nms. Accessed 11 Mar 2019

Language and literature (2019) SAGE Publications Inc. https://us.sagepub.com/en-us/cam/journal/language-and-literature. Accessed 07 Mar 2019

Language Realm (2014) Your free resource for language and translation services. http://www.languagerealm.com/. Accessed 08 Mar 2019

Language teaching (2017) Cambridge Core. https://www.cambridge.org/core/journals/language-teaching. Accessed 08 Mar 2019

Law probability and risk (2019) Oxford Academic. https://academic.oup.com/lpr. Accessed 08 Mar 2019

Learning and instruction (2019) Journal—Elsevier. https://www.journals.elsevier.com/learning-and-instruction. Accessed 08 Mar 2019

LegisMac (2014) University of Macau—Wu Yee Sun Library. http://library.umac.mo/html/databases/e_databases.asp. Accessed 08 Mar 2019

Lexis.com (2014) University of Macau—Wu Yee Sun Library https://library.umac.mo/html/databases/e_databases.asp. Accessed 08 Mar 2019

Literature online (2014) University of Macau—Wu Yee Sun Library. https://library.umac.mo/html/databases/e_databases_id_res.asp?getsuid=6. Accessed 07 Mar 2019

Macao's External Merchandise Trade Statistics Database (2017) DSEC. https://www.dsec.gov.mo/NCEM.aspx. Accessed 08 Mar 2019

Macau Government Printing Bureau (2019) Home. https://www.io.gov.mo/cn/home/. Accessed 08 Mar 2019

Modern Chinese literature and culture (2019) JSTOR: modern Chinese literature and culture. https://www.jstor.org/journal/modechinlitecult?item_view=journal_info. Accessed 08 Mar 2019

Monetary Authority of Macao (2019). https://www.amcm.gov.mo/en/about-amcm/history. Accessed 08 Mar 2019

oTranscribe (2019). https://otranscribe.com/. Accessed 08 Mar 2019

Parry and Grant Encyclopaedic Dictionary of International Law (2014) University of Macau—Wu Yee Sun Library. https://library.umac.mo/html/databases/e_databases.asp. Accessed 08 Mar 2019

Personality and social psychology review (2019)Personality and Social Psychology Review | SAGE Publications Ltd. https://uk.sagepub.com/en-gb/asi/journal/personality-and-social-psychology-review. Accessed 11 Mar 2019

Philosopher's Index (2014) University of Macau—Wu Yee Sun Library. https://library.umac.mo/html/databases/e_databases_id_res.asp?getsuid=6. Accessed 07 Mar 2019

Political, Economic, and Military Conditions in China (2014) University of Macau—Wu Yee Sun Library. http://library.umac.mo/html/databases/e_databases.asp. Accessed 08 Mar 2019

Political, Economic, and Military Conditions in China: Reports and Correspondence of the U.S. (2011) Military Intelligence Division, 1918–1941.—Version details—Trove. https://trove.nla.gov.au/work/211287035?q&versionId=232008001. Accessed 08 Mar 2019

ProQuest criminal justice (2019) About—criminal justice database—LibGuides at ProQuest. https://proquest.libguides.com/criminaljusticedatabase. Accessed 08 Mar 2019

ProQuest Military Collection (2014) University of Macau—Wu Yee Sun Library. http://library.umac.mo/html/databases/e_databases.asp. Accessed 08 Mar 2019

ProQuest Political Science (2019) About—Political Science Database—LibGuides at ProQuest. https://proquest.libguides.com/politicalsciencedatabase. Accessed 08 Mar 2019

ProQuest Social Science Journals (2019) About—Social Science Database—LibGuides at ProQuest. https://proquest.libguides.com/socialsciencedatabase. Accessed 08 Mar 2019

PsycARTICLES (2019) Home. https://www.apa.org/pubs/databases/psycarticles. Accessed 08 Mar 2019

PsycBooks (2019) PsycBOOKS. https://www.apa.org/pubs/databases/psycbooks. Accessed 08 Mar 2019

PsycInfo (2014) University of Macau—Wu Yee Sun Library. http://library.umac.mo/html/databases/e_databases.asp. Accessed 08 Mar 2019

Psychology crime and law (2018) Psychology, Crime & Law—Wikipedia. https://en.wikipedia.org/wiki/Psychology,_Crime_%26_Law. Accessed 08 Mar 2019

Public administration review (2019) Public Administration | Public Policy & Administration | General & Introductory Political Science | Subjects | Wiley. https://www.wiley.com/en-us/Public+Administration+Review-p-9780JRNL67076. Accessed 11 Mar 2019

Publications of Macao Special Administrative Region Legislative Assembly (2017) Introduction. http://www.al.gov.mo/en/. Accessed 08 Mar 2019

Quarterly journal of economics (2019) Oxford academic. https://academic.oup.com/qje/pages/About. Accessed 08 Mar 2019

Review of education research (2018) SAGE Publications. https://us.sagepub.com/en-us/nam/review-of-educational-research/journal201854. Accessed 08 Mar 2019

Service and Products (2017) DSEC. https://www.dsec.gov.mo/ServicesAndProducts.aspx?lang=en-US. Accessed 08 Mar 2019

Social issues and policy review (2019)SPSSI Journals. https://spssi.onlinelibrary.wiley.com/hub/journal/17512409/aims-and-scope/read-full-aims-and-scope. Accessed 11 Mar 2019

Sociological methods and research (2019)- Journal Resources for Authors—Michigan PSC. https://www.psc.isr.umich.edu/dis/infoserv/journal/detail/1167. Accessed 11 Mar 2019

Stanford law review (2018) Wikipedia. https://en.wikipedia.org/wiki/Stanford_Law_Review. Accessed 08 Mar 2019

Studies in second language acquisition (2018) Cambridge Core. https://www.cambridge.org/core/journals/studies-in-second-language-acquisition. Accessed 07 Mar 2019

The Centre for Law Studies publications (2018) Faculty of Law. https://fll.um.edu.mo/research/centre-for-law-studies/. Accessed 08 Mar 2019

The Hong Kong Education Bibliographic Database (2014) University of Macau—Wu Yee Sun Library. https://library.umac.mo/html/databases/e_databases.asp. Accessed 08 Mar 2019

The making of modern law: foreign, comparative, and international law (2012) 1600–1926 [electronic resource]. in SearchWorks catalog. https://searchworks.stanford.edu/view/9700213. Accessed 08 Mar 2019

The Modern Language Journal (2019) JSTOR. https://www.jstor.org/journal/modernlanguagej?item_view=journal_info. Accessed 08 Mar 2019

The Times Digital Archive (2014) 1785–2011 (The Times (London)). https://www.galileo.usg.edu/scholar/gcsu/databases/timi-geo1/. Accessed 08 Mar 2019

The Yale Law Journal (2019) Wikipedia. https://en.wikipedia.org/wiki/Yale_Law_Journal. Accessed 08 Mar 2019

TOMEDES About Us (2019) Upcoming translation conference. https://www.tomedes.com/about-tomedes. Accessed 08 Mar 2019

Topics in early childhood special education (2019) SAGE Journals. https://journals.sagepub.com/home/tec. Accessed 08 Mar 2019

Translation and interpreting studies (2019) The Journal of the American Translation and Interpreting Studies Association | John Benjamins. https://www.jbe-platform.com/content/journals/18762700. Accessed 07 Mar 2019

Translation studies bibliography (TSB) University of Macau—Wu Yee Sun Library. https://library.umac.mo/html/databases/e_databases_id_res.asp?getsuid=6. Accessed 07 Mar 2019

UM Macau Studies Databases (2014) Home. http://libdigital.umac.mo/was5/digital/macau_study.jsp. Accessed 11 Mar 2019

Virtual Library of Macau (2018) About. https://www.macaudata.com/indexaction/about?headType=9. Accessed 11 Mar 2019

Web Gallery of art (2019) Web gallery of art, image collection, virtual museum, searchable database of European fine arts (200–1900). https://www.wga.hu/welcome_m.html. Accessed 07 Mar 2019

Westlaw China (2019) Westlaw China. http://www.westlawchina.com/index_en.html. Accessed 08 Mar 2019

Wind 資訊 (金融終端及經濟數據終端) (2011) Wind 资讯--产品信息. https://www.wind.com.cn/product/Wind.WBT.html. Accessed 08 Mar 2019

WorldLingo Free Translation Online (2018) Tools—translation/transliteration resources—LibGuides at California Institute of Technology. https://libguides.caltech.edu/c.php?g=512667&p=5330098. Accessed 08 Mar 2019

WorldTradeLaw (2019) WorldTradeLaw.net. http://www.worldtradelaw.net/. Accessed 08 Mar 2019

澳門大學圖書館古籍特藏圖錄 (2014) University of Macau—Wu Yee Sun Library. https://library.umac.mo/html/databases/e_databases_id_res.asp?getsuid=6. Accessed 07 Mar 2019

國學寶典 (2014) University of Macau—Wu Yee Sun Library. https://library.umac.mo/html/databases/e_databases_id_res.asp?getsuid=6. Accessed 07 Mar 2019

北大法意 (2019) 法意科技. http://www.lawyee.com/. Accessed 08 Mar 2019

北大法寶 (2018) 產品與服務. http://www.pkulaw.cn/help/chanpin/chanpin1_1.aspx. Accessed 08 Mar 2019

法源法律網 (2014) University of Macau—Wu Yee Sun Library. https://library.umac.mo/html/databases/e_databases.asp. Accessed 08 Mar 2019

萬律 (2019) 法律信息检索 - 法律法规双语在线数据库 – 万律中国. http://www.westlawchina.com/index_cn.html. Accessed 08 Mar 2019

香港影評庫 (2019) 簡介 | 香港影評庫. https://www.filmcritics.org.hk/film-review/about. Accessed 08 Mar 2019

Chapter 7
Search Engines

Abstract Search engines are designed to help people find information stored on the Internet. They enable users to find needed information across billions of web pages with relatively little efforts. This chapter introduces the types of search engines and the reuse of Chinese and Western search engines.

7.1 Types of Search Engines

Search engines generally fall into the following types:

- Crawler-based search engines, such as Google, which creates its database automatically by special programs called crawlers or spiders. The crawler digs through individual web pages, pulls out keywords and then adds the pages to the search engine's database;
- Human-powered directories such as the Open Directory, which uses human expertise to list web pages. A website is submitted to the directory and must be approved for inclusion by editorial staff;
- Hybrid search engines, which involve both crawler- and human-selected sites.

7.2 Integrated Search Engines

Integrated search engines are also called "meta" search engines, with "meta" meaning to "go beyond." These are particularly useful, since they search several search engines at once and combine the results. While you get more results with integrated search engines, the relevancy and quality of the results may sometimes suffer. You will need to carefully review the results and also know how best to search so you get relevant and useful results.

Examples of integrated search engines include Dogpile (www.dogpile.com), MetaCrawler (www.metacrawler.com), and SavvySearch (SavvySearch).

B. T. H. Leung et al., *Transferring Information Literacy Practices*,
https://doi.org/10.1007/978-981-13-7743-3_7

7.3 Chinese Language Academic Search Engines

7.3.1 Baidu Scholar

In 2014, Baidu launched Baidu Scholar with the aim of becoming the biggest, most comprehensive research platform in China. By the end of 2018, Baidu Scholar included hundreds of thousands of academic websites with an index of over 400 million literature resources, thus providing free access to a huge amount of Chinese and foreign literature. For scholars working with Chinese subjects or limited to Chinese as their working language, Baidu is particularly useful. Note that the interface of Baidu Scholar is only available in Chinese.

7.3.1.1 Searching in Baidu Scholar

For basic searches, simply type search terms in the search box. For Advanced searches, click the icon at the right corner of the search box. While advanced search options are not as detailed in Baidu as with academic databases, users can search by title, author, or use Boolean search terms (see Chap. 2) (Fig. 7.1).

7.3.1.2 Search Results

Baidu Scholar provides multiple options so you can refine and filter results. For example, you can narrow or limit results by date, subject, key words, content type, author, institution, and so on.

Fig. 7.1 Main page of Baidu Scholar (http://xueshu.baidu.com/)

Search results are listed in the middle column. At the end of each record are quick links to save, cite, or download the article.

The right column lists additional related resources. These include research topic analysis, related popular search terms, and more (Fig. 7.2).

Figure 7.3 is an example of details for an article with listings of full text sources (including free full text links). Baidu also gives you similar articles, reference lists, etc.

7.3.1.3 Scholar Metrics and Chinese Academic Journal Metrics

Baidu Scholar also provides "metrics" to help users to evaluate the visibility and influence of the sources they locate. For example, they tell us the reach and influence of particular scholars and Chinese academic journals. These statistics (metrics) help you to evaluate which sources are best. Metrics can be found at the bottom of each Baidu Scholar homepage (Fig. 7.4).

7.3.1.4 Benefits of Creating a Baidu Scholar Account

Baidu Scholar can help you set up keyword search alerts. When new content is available that matches a keyword search query you have made, a search alert automatically notifies your Baidu Scholar account. This is wonderful tool for

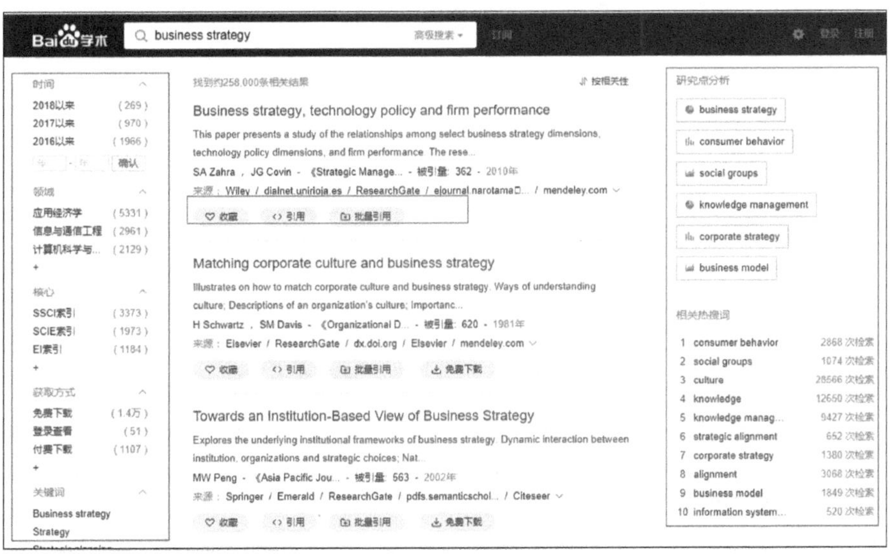

Fig. 7.2 Search result page of Baidu Scholar (http://xueshu.baidu.com/s?wd=business+strategy)

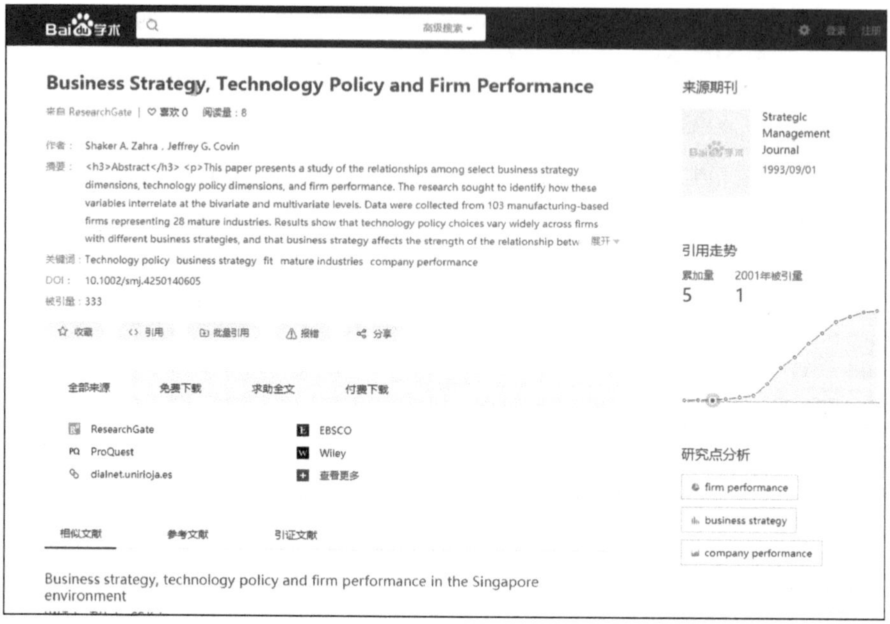

Fig. 7.3 Detailed record page of Baidu Scholar (http://xueshu.baidu.com/usercenter/paper/show)

Fig. 7.4 Baidu Scholar main page with Scholar metrics and Chinese academic journal metrics highlighted (http://xueshu.baidu.com/)

scholars working for a long time in a particular research area and helps them to keep up with new information and publications in their specialty area.

Another great feature of having a Baidu Scholar account is that you can save articles (Fig. 7.5).

7.4 Western Language Academic Search Engines

7.4.1 Google Scholar

Google Scholar is a freely-accessible web search engine that indexes the full text or metadata of scholarly literature across many publishing formats and disciplines. You will find it extremely useful if working in English. For example, Google Scholar includes journal and conference papers, theses and dissertations, academic books, abstracts, technical reports, etc. from numerous areas of research.

Google Scholar may also be accessible from a basic Google search results page on your computer. Simply select the link inside the red box (see Fig. 7.6) to access scholarly article results.

7.4.1.1 Basic Scholar Search

Searching Google Scholar is very similar to general Google searching using topic (keyword) searches.

Fig. 7.5 Baidu Scholar main page with personal account highlighted (http://xueshu.baidu.com/)

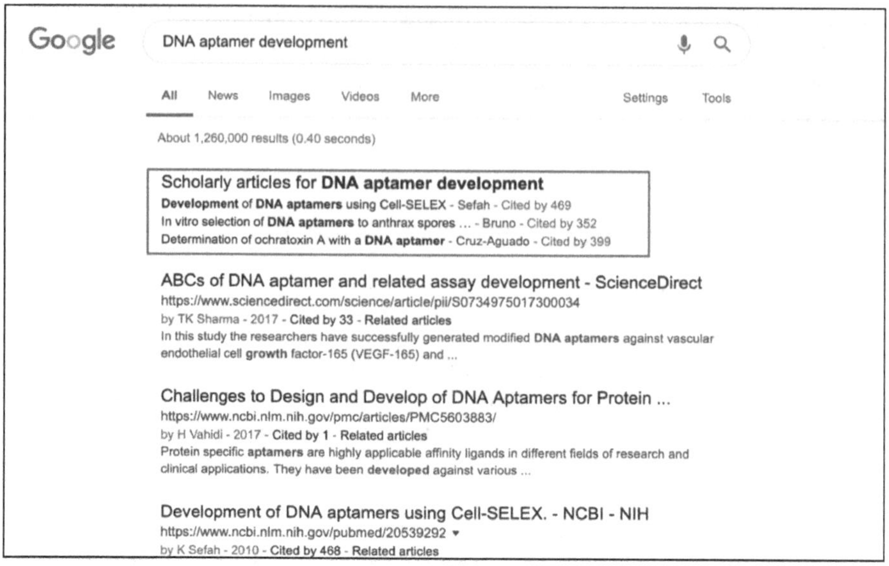

Fig. 7.6 Google Scholar search result page (https://scholar.google.com/scholar?hl=en)

If the item is from an Open Access source or if the UM library has an institutional subscription to that journal, you will be able to download the entire article (full-text). If you can't find a link to the full-text article, try searching for the journal in our UM library catalogue.

7.4.1.2 Advanced Scholar Search

Google Scholar provides basic and advanced searches. To conduct Advanced searches, click the icon at the top left corner, selectin Advanced Search (Fig. 7.7).

Please note that, in Google Scholar, advanced search options are limited compared with academic databases. Also, Boolean searches are available in a different format. You are able to limit your search by title, author, etc. (Fig. 7.8).

7.4.1.3 Google Scholar Search Results

On the result page, use the options on the left column to limit results by time, or sort results by relevance or date (more vs. less current sources).

The title link of a record will take you to the publisher's website where the article has been published. If the article is available in our university library, you will see a full text link to the right of the record, showing the university's web domain (Fig. 7.9).

Fig. 7.7 Link to Google Scholar advanced search (https://scholar.google.com/schhp?hl=en&as_sdt=0,5#d=gs_hdr_drw)

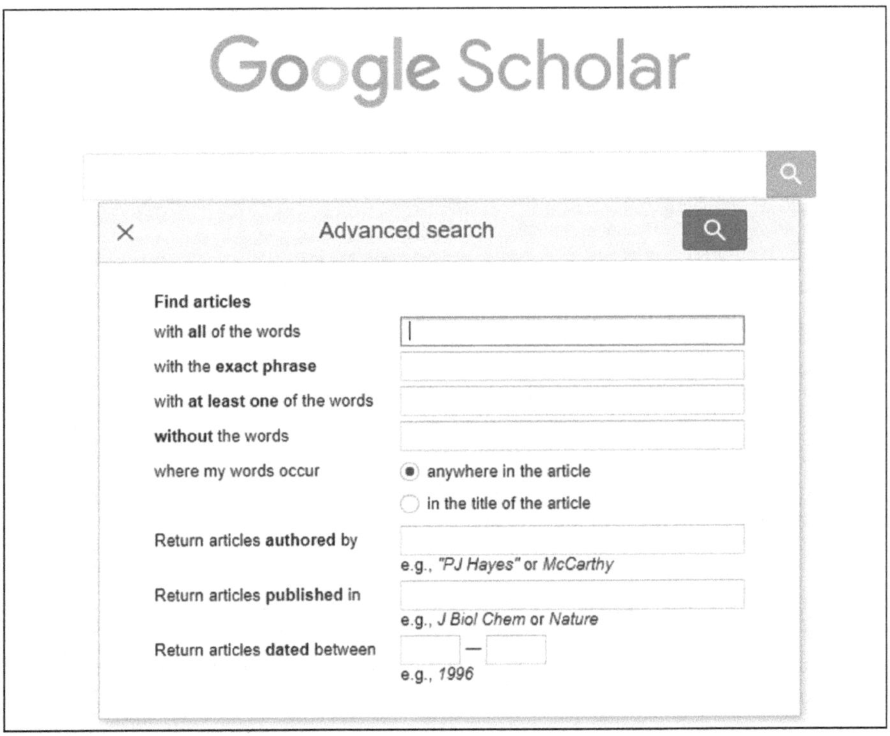

Fig. 7.8 Google Scholar advanced search option (https://scholar.google.com/schhp?hl=en&as_sdt=0,5#d=gs_asd)

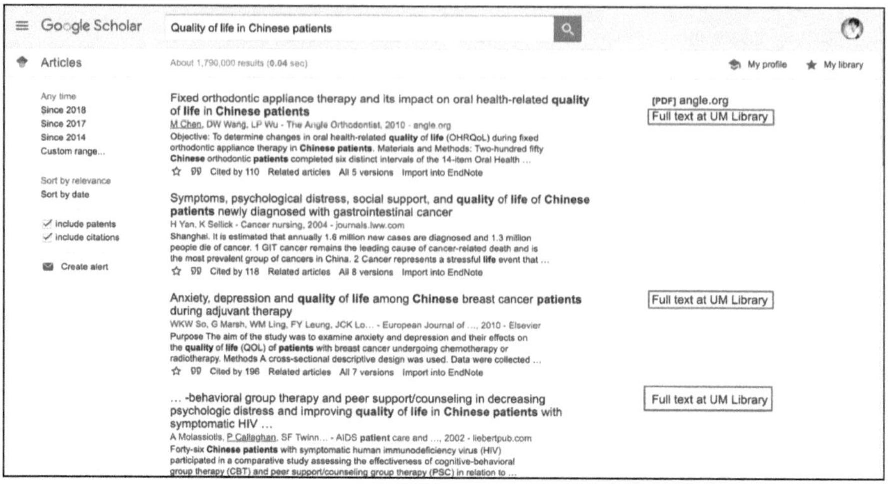

Fig. 7.9 Google Scholar search result page with "Full Text at UM Library" highlighted (https://scholar.google.com/scholar?hl=en&as_sdt=0%2C5&q=Quality+of+life+in+chinese+patients&oq=Quality+of+life+in+Chinese+patie)

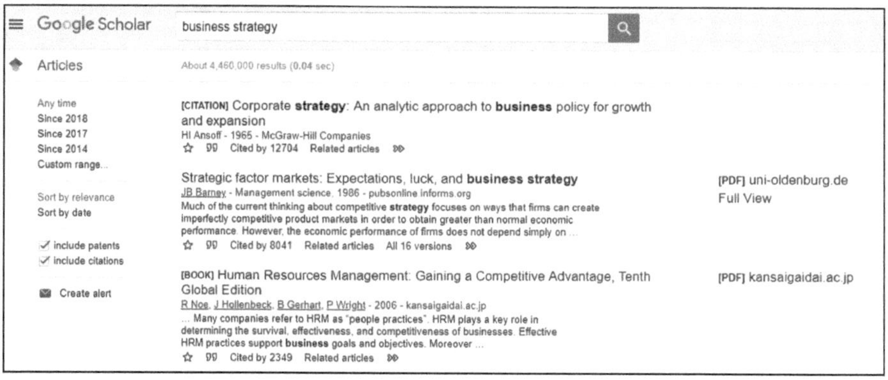

Fig. 7.10 Google Scholar search result page with only free full text (https://scholar.google.com/scholar?hl=en&as_sdt=0%2C5&q=business+strategy&btnG=)

A full text link will appear in the right column, too, which means a free copy is available.

The buttons at the end of a record allow you to save, cite, or locate more (related) resources (Fig. 7.10).

7.4.1.4 Google Scholar Metrics

Click on author name(s) in a record to go to the Google Scholar Metrics page.

Google Scholar Metrics provide an easy way for us to quickly decide the visibility and influence of recent scholarly articles. Scholar Metrics summarize recent citations to many publications. Besides helping users to understand the influence of scholars, this also helps professors and other researchers as they consider where to try to publish their new research (Fig. 7.11).

7.4.1.5 Google Scholar Account

It is a good idea to create a Google account so you can save the most useful or important articles you have found (Fig. 7.12).

7.4.1.6 Additional Hints

When an author or source repeatedly appears in your results, try searching for publications just by that author. Retain keywords of your choice, such as "aptamer." To do this, use the 'author:' operator and add a name such as "Waihong Tan" with quotation marks (Fig. 7.13).

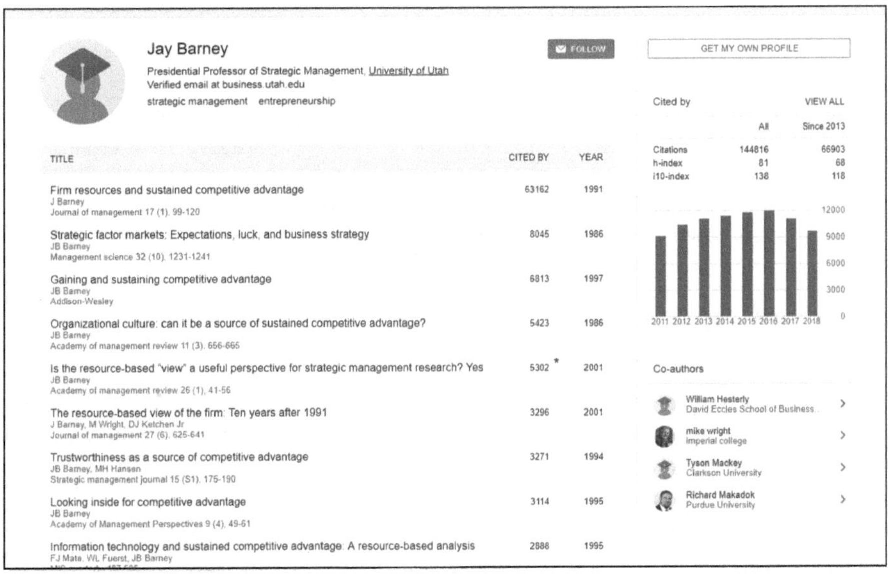

Fig. 7.11 An example of Google Scholar Matrix (https://scholar.google.com/citations?hl=en&user=vGSZsWcAAAAJ)

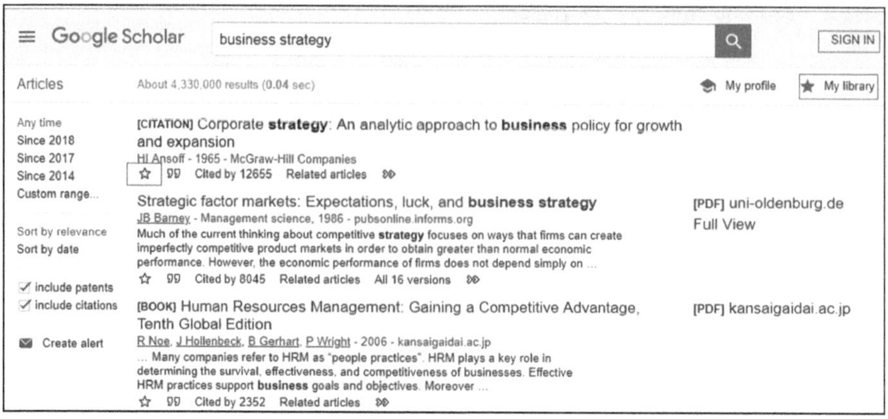

Fig. 7.12 An example of Google Scholar personal account (https://scholar.google.com/scholar?hl=en&as_sdt=0%2C5&q=business+strategy&btnG=)

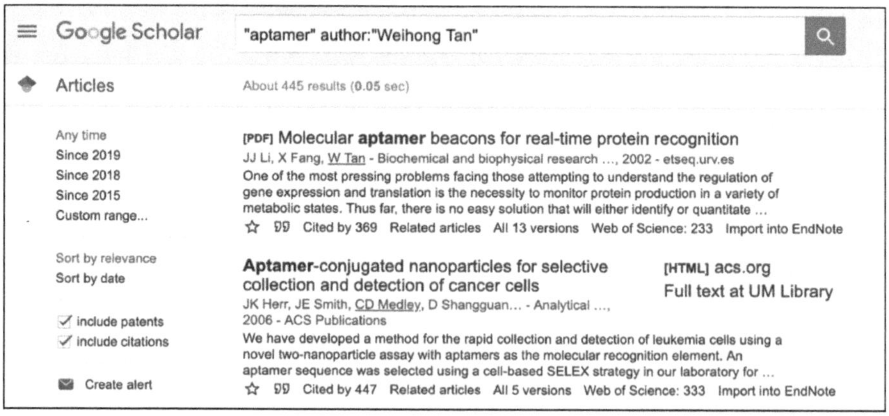

Fig. 7.13 An example of Google Scholar additional search hints (https://scholar.google.com/scholar?hl=en&as_sdt=0%2C5&q=%22aptamer%22+author%3A%22Weihong+Tan%22&btnG=)

7.5 Artificial Intelligence and the Future Search Engines

At the LeWeb conference in 2013, Google Engineering Director Scott Huffman introduced the direction of Google's search business. He believes that Google's future goal is to develop the ultimate personal assistant service (Google Wants To Build The Ultimate Personal Assistant (2013)).

In the next few years, smart speaker products represented by Google Home and Amazon Echo, he says, will be maturing and having an impact on web-based searches. Some of the features that future search engines will likely have are listed below.

7.5.1 Voice Searches

The number of voice searches has risen dramatically to the point where voice search, rather than being a novelty, is practically a new standard. Users can use basic phrases to search for content, and need not decide specific keywords to include when making queries.

7.5.2 Casual Searches

Mobile devices make searching easier, giving users access to almost any search engine anytime, anywhere. Using smart speakers, we don't even have to use our fingers to search. This level of convenience will increase the number of searches used by search engines and dramatically change the content of what people search for. On-demand searches will be more frequent and more likely to meet immediate user needs.

7.5.3 No Screen Search

With the exception of a few devices, today's smart speakers do not use traditional screen interfaces. They need not rely on interactions on screen to get results; instead, we can just talk to the digital assistant. This will dramatically change traditional search engine results and may help us reconsider the visibility and ranking of search results.

7.5.4 IoT Interactions

As the Internet of Things (IoT) is applied more extensively to lifestyle and workplace scenarios, we will see the emergence of more connected devices and have more search engine data than ever before. For example, Windows Cortana is a breakthrough technology that allows users to search both local machines and the Internet. Smart speakers allow users to instantly search and interact with any connected device in the home. This will greatly expand our data accessibility and service channels.

7.5.5 Personalized Searching

Smart speakers thus will be able to collect more user data than ever before, leveraging multiple devices, multiple accounts, and a large number of home-based search histories and habits. This allows more personalization and customization, mean more relevant, tailored results for each search.

Reference

Google Wants To Build The Ultimate Personal Assistant (2013) TechCrunch. https://techcrunch.com/2013/12/25/google-wants-to-build-the-ultimate-personal-assistant/. Accessed 08 Mar 2019

Chapter 8
Developing Information Literacy Skills with Various Tools

Abstract Information literacy is an ability to use information technology so as to acquire information, to evaluate it and to use it in our study, work and everyday lives. There are various kinds of tools to enable and enhance information literacy, as a process or as a skill. We discuss some of the most commonly-used ones in this chapter.

8.1 Information Literacy Tools

Nowadays, anytime and anywhere, people access the Internet for information. They browse news, read articles and online books, watch films, do surveys, share ideas, publish works and do other activities on the Internet. Do they know how to use search techniques/tools to implement these activities? For example, many people like searching on Google with certain keywords for the websites they want to browse, instead of typing the urls of the websites on the browsers. Some people may like to view the ppt files on SlideShare to learn about the development of big data instead of reading books or articles with long texts. Some may create simple online forms for their friends to fill in so as to set up a suitable party time. The following sections list 5 types of tools for information literacy. Perhaps you already know some of them.

8.1.1 Featured Contents Tools

Our most recent online searches might include an address of a restaurant, picture of a famous person, a travel video, a book, a journal article, most recent Twitter release from celebrities, or something we weren't yet able to find. One-stop search tools like Google, Baidu (百度), or Bing may help. But they return a huge number of results, making it necessary to tediously evaluate to locate the most reliable information.

B. T. H. Leung et al., *Transferring Information Literacy Practices*,
https://doi.org/10.1007/978-981-13-7743-3_8

In Chaps. 2–7 of this book, you have learnt a number of reliable tools and databases for getting academic resources for various subjects and special topics. In this section, some commonly used tools for featured, authorized or unique contents are shared with you.

- **WorldCat for Bibliographic Data Worldwide**

WorldCat is the world's largest network of library contents and services. It includes the bibliographic information from thousands of library members in more than 100 countries. With this online bibliographic tool, you are enabled to find a book and locate it in your nearest libraries. This service also has a paid version, accessing more comprehensive bibliographic data (Figs. 8.1 and 8.2).

- **SlideShare for Professional Contents**

As shown in Fig. 8.3, SlideShare enables its users to discover, share and learn through presentations, infographics, and other documents. It is a large professional content sharing community.

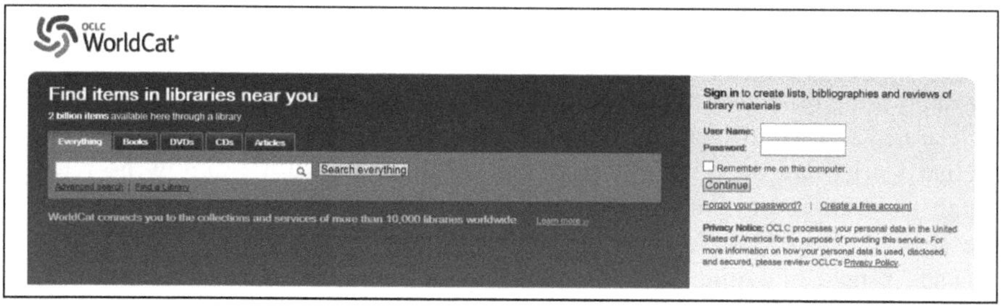

Fig. 8.1 WorldCat search page (www.worldcat.org)

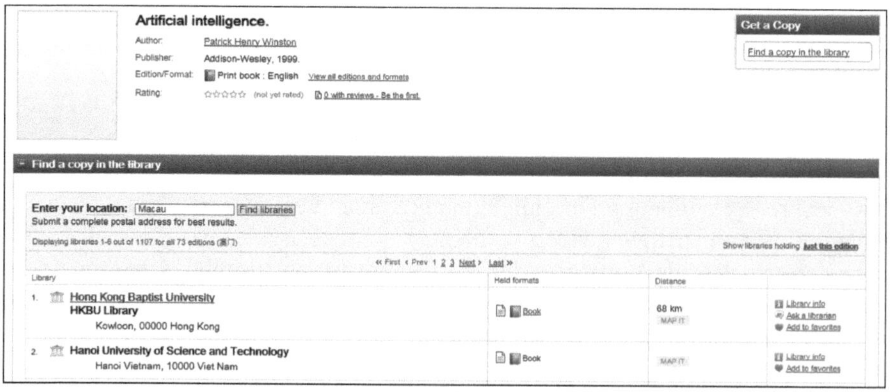

Fig. 8.2 The nearest libraries listed for the selected item in WorldCat (www.worldcat.org)

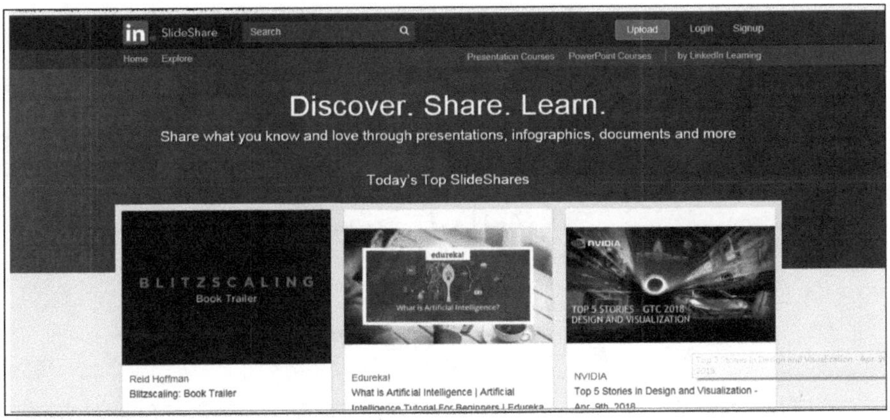

Fig. 8.3 SlideShare website (www.slideshare.net)

Fig. 8.4 Internet archive search page (https://archive.org)

- **Internet Archive, a Free Digital Library with Archived Web Pages**

Internet Archive is a non-profit digital library offering free universal access to books, movies and music, as well as billions of archived web pages. Its Wayback Machine allows you to explore a particular website dating back to 2001 (Figs. 8.4 and 8.5).

- **HathiTrust, a Digital Preservation Repository**

HathiTrust Digital Library provides long-term preservation and access services freely to digitized content from a variety of sources, including Google, the Internet Archive, Microsoft, and in-house member institution initiatives. It covers a collection of millions of titles digitized from libraries around the world (Fig. 8.6).

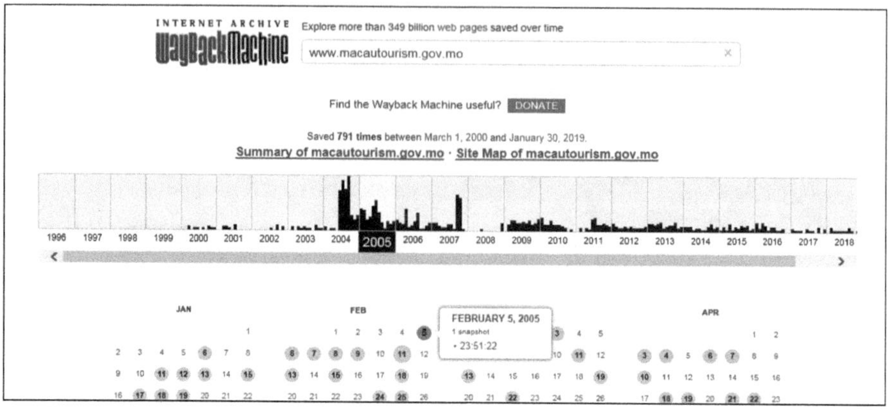

Fig. 8.5 Wayback Machine on Internet Archive (www.archive.org/web)

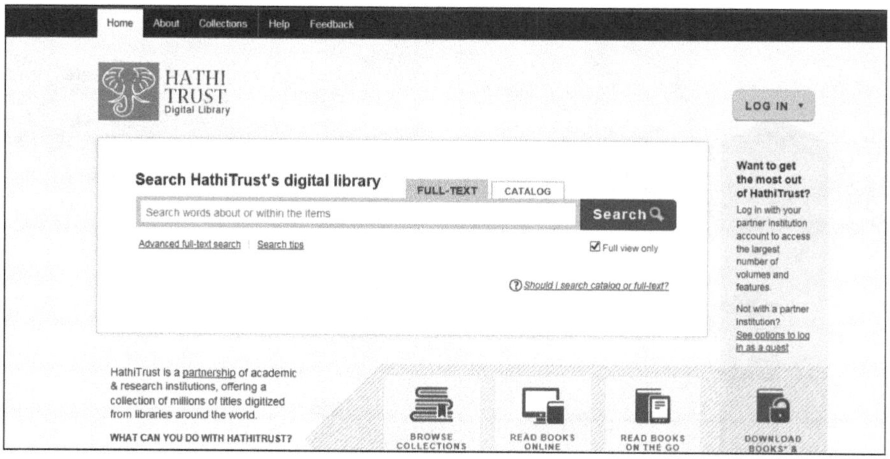

Fig. 8.6 HathiTrust digital library search page (www.hathitrust.org/digital_library)

Most archival works on HathiTrust Digital Library are in the public domain or have necessary permissions for free access. Do you know the minimum duration of protection of works? According to the Berne Convention for the Protection of Literary and Artistic Works (1886),[1] the general rule to the duration of protection is that protection must be granted until the expiration of the 50th year after the author's death. As for audiovisual (cinematographic) works, the duration of protection is 50 years after the release of the work to the public. For applied art and photographic works, it is 25 years after the creation of the work.

[1]Source: https://www.wipo.int/treaties/en/ip/berne/summary_berne.html.

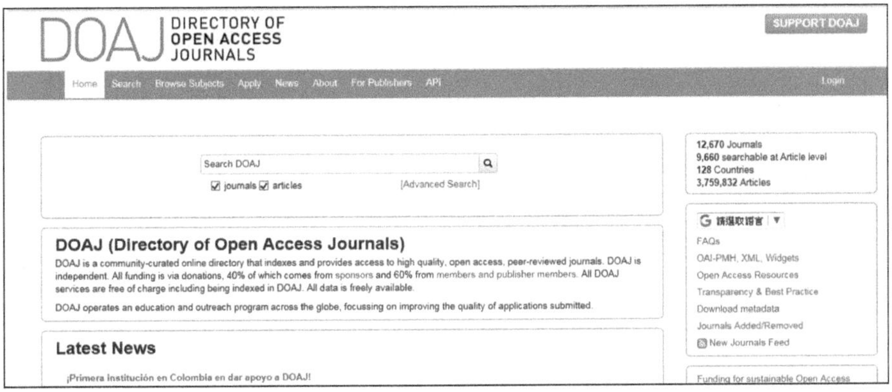

Fig. 8.7 DOAJ website (www.doaj.org/)

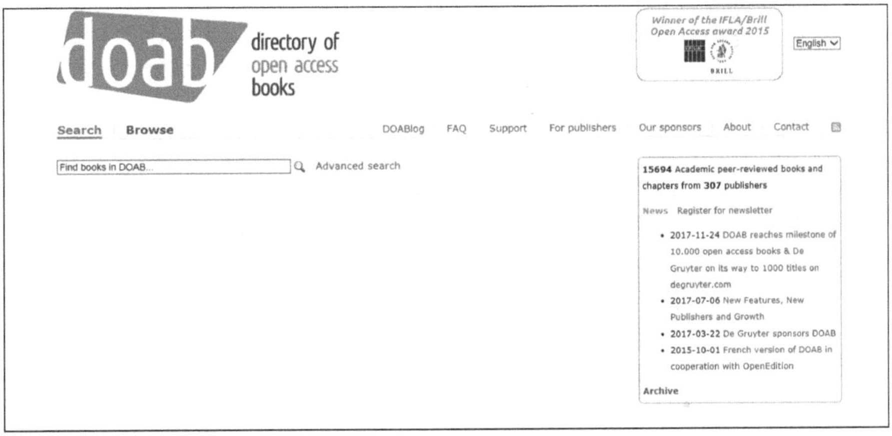

Fig. 8.8 DOAB website (www.doabooks.org)

- **Directory of Open Access Journals (DOAJ), a Free E-Journals Platform**

DOAJ is a community-curated online directory that indexes and provides access to high quality, open access,[2] peer-reviewed journals. It includes nearly 13,000 open access journals with 4 million articles from about 130 countries (Fig. 8.7).

- **Directory of Open Access Books (DOAB), a Free E-Books Platform**

Aiming at increasing discoverability of open access books, DOAB provides access to nearly 16,000 academic peer-reviewed books and chapters from 307 publishers (Fig. 8.8).

[2]Open Access is a practice born in digital age. Open access contents could be freely accessed by anyone on the Internet.

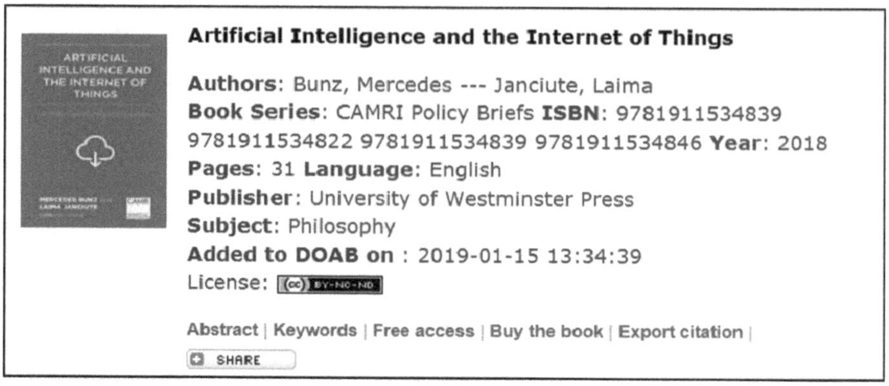

Fig. 8.9 A book record on DOAB (www.doabooks.org)

There is a field "License" included in each book/chapter record in DOAB stating the Creative Commons (CC) license under which the relevant work is protected. The CC copyright licenses provide a simply and standardized way for you to grant copyright permissions of your creative work to publish online. Others could then share and use your work on conditions of your choice. The CC licenses have been widely used all around the world to share creative works on the Internet (Fig. 8.9).

The following lists the 4 license conditions[3] of CC license:

Attribution (by)

All CC licenses require that others who use your work in any way must give you credit the way you request, but not in a way that suggests you endorse them or their use. If they want to use your work without giving you credit or for endorsement purposes, they must get your permission first

ShareAlike (sa)

You let others copy, distribute, display, perform, and modify your work, as long as they distribute any modified work on the same terms. If they want to distribute modified works under other terms, they must get your permission first

NonCommercial (nc)

You let others copy, distribute, display, perform, and (unless you have chosen NoDerivatives) modify and use your work for any purpose other than commercially unless they get your permission first

NoDerivatives (nd)

You let others copy, distribute, display and perform only original copies of your work. If they want to modify your work, they must get your permission first

[3]Source: https://creativecommons.org/share-your-work/licensing-types-examples/.

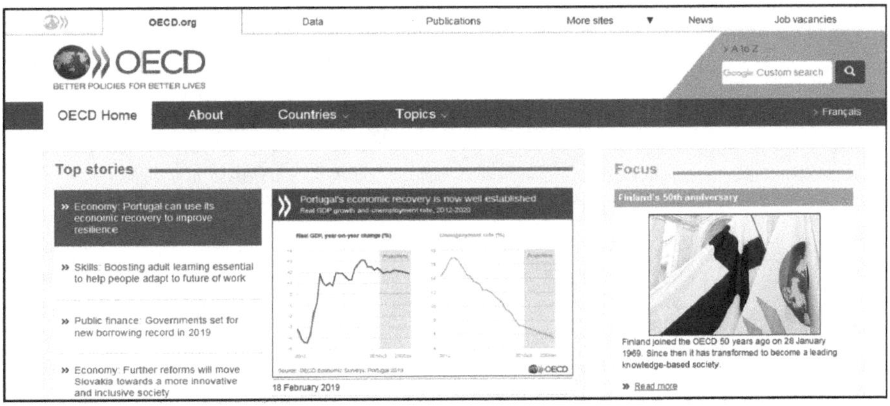

Fig. 8.10 OECD website (www.oecd.org)

To further understand the conditions and remix of the CC licenses and publish your work with them, please go and have a try at https://creativecommons.org/share-your-work/licensing-types-examples/.

- **OECD.org for International Statistics and Reports**

Many international organizations provide statistics and reports on their websites free of charge. OECD is one of them and an important one. It provides information on a broad range of topics to help governments foster prosperity and fight poverty through economic growth and financial stability. On its platform, you may browse by country or topic for relevant data and reports. OECD iLibrary, a subscription service, covers a full range of OECD contents (Fig. 8.10).

PISA is the OECD's Program for International Student Assessment. It tests 15-year-old students from all over the world in reading, mathematics and sciences every three years. The results and information of PISA can also be found on the OECD.org website (Fig. 8.11).

- **Social Media as Search Tools**

As you well know, nowadays people share information and knowledge on social media anytime and anywhere. Celebrities release their news on social media like Twitter, Facebook, WeChat, Instagram, YouTube and so on. To trace real-time information of this kind, you may follow or search on social media (Fig. 8.12).

8.1.2 Online Surveys and Questionnaires Tools

Online surveys and questionnaires are a simply and cost-effective way to get in touch with the targeted audience and collect feedback. There are a variety of online surveys tools available on the Internet. This section introduces several you may find useful when doing surveys and questionnaires.

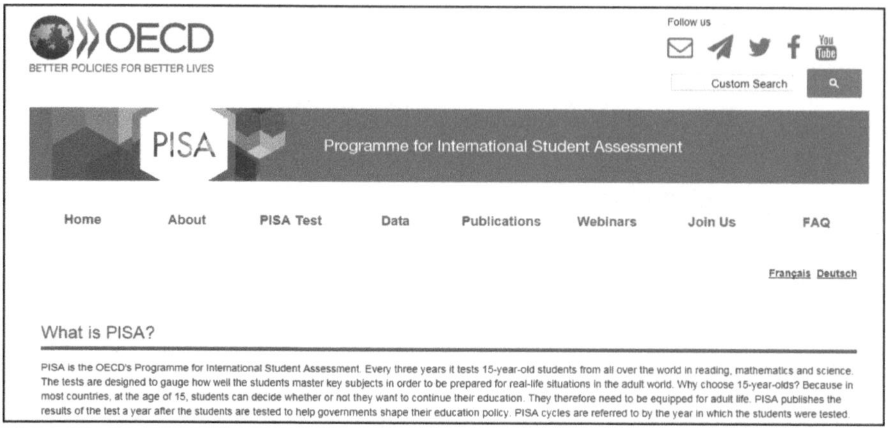

Fig. 8.11 PISA website (www.oecd.org/pisa)

Fig. 8.12 Harry Potter Film's Twitter page (www.twitter.com)

- **Google Forms**

Google Forms helps you design surveys, conduct them, and analyze the results. It is an easy tool to collect and organize information online free of charge. A step-by-step guide leads you through the entire setting-up process. You may start a new form or choose from a template gallery to make a form. Your questions can be multiple choice, open-ended questions, linear scale or other styles. After setting the questions, the form is ready to be sent out. You can then collect and analyze the results, also using Google Forms to show organized responses (Figs. 8.13 and 8.14).

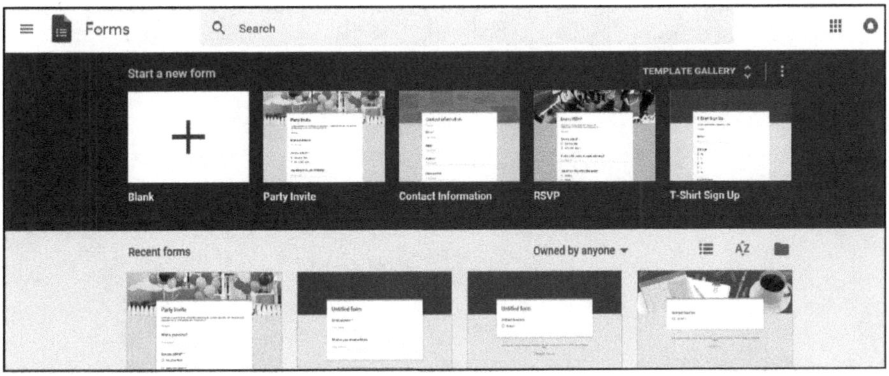

Fig. 8.13 Start a form on Google forms (www.google.com/forms)

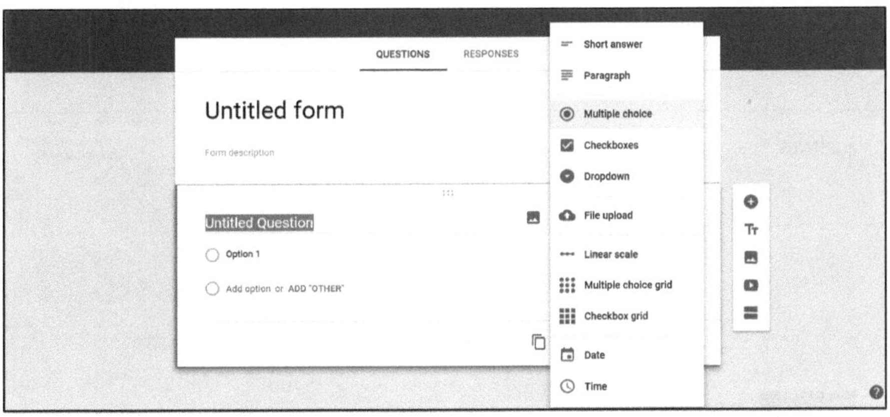

Fig. 8.14 Create various kinds of questions on Google forms (www.google.com/forms)

- **Survey Monkey**

This is a popular tool for creating surveys using format. A variety of question templates are available. You set up your survey, add questions, send surveys and analyze results. The Survey Monkey basic version is free, with an enhanced version available at a cost (Fig. 8.15).

- **Qualtrics**

Qualtrics is a paid web-based survey service, used by 9,000 + businesses and institutions worldwide. It allows users to build customer profiles, create surveys and work for sophisticated global experience management solutions, while supporting academic research (Fig. 8.16).

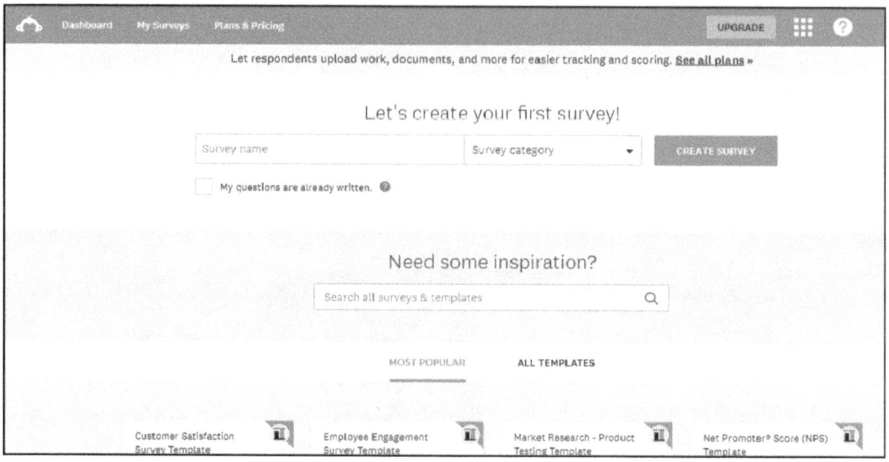

Fig. 8.15 Starting page after free log-in on survey monkey (www.surveymonkey.com)

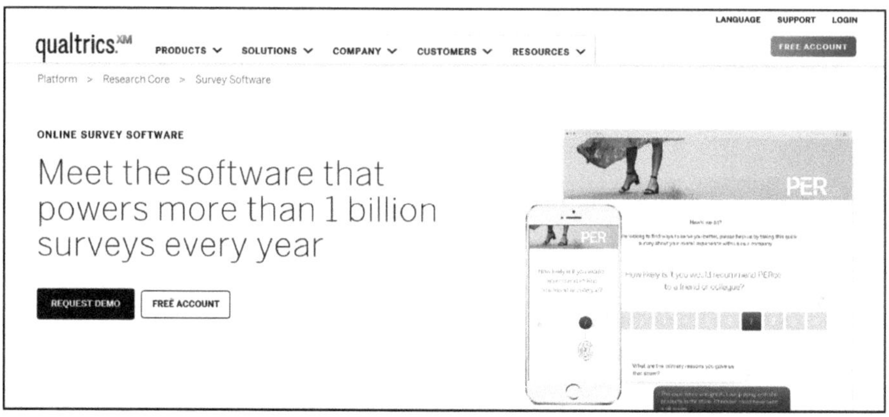

Fig. 8.16 Qualtrics website (www.qualtrics.com/research-core/survey-software/)

8.1.3 Citation Analysis Tools

Citation analysis can be used to examine research trends, patterns and inter-actions. Used especially in scientific and some social sciences fields, citation analysis can help to better understand the research quality and to detect emerging research trends. It can also help to find important and classic readings in a particular subject. This section introduces several useful tools and their distinguishing metrics and features.

8.1.3.1 Web of Science Tools

- **Web of Science Core Collection**

Web of Science (WoS) provides citation information to over 18,000 world's leading and high impact journals, 180,000 conference proceedings, and over 80,000 books from around the world. The titles included in WoS are rigorously selected and reflect the current academic status worldwide.

You may search the topic you are interested in on WoS. By exploring the cited and citing information of a certain relevant article, you can further expand or narrow your research (Fig. 8.17).

- **Journal Citation Report**
  (www.clarivate.com/products/journal-citation-reports/)

Journal Citation Report (JCR) was the first tool worldwide for in-depth analyses and ranking of research and professional journals. JCR, a paid service, provides a quantitative tool called "Impact Factor" (IF) to compare the academic impact of journals in the same subject categories. The higher the value of IF, the more influential the journal. By using the citation data from WoS, IF is a measure of the frequency with which the "average article" in a journal has been cited in a particular year or period. It is not recommended to compare the IF among journals in different subject categories, as there is a significant difference on the citation patterns among different subject categories (Fig. 8.18).

In general, a journal covered by WoS has been considered of high quality. It should be a good journal for consulting and publishing papers. A full master list of journals covered by WoS could be found at http://mjl.clarivate.com/.

- **InCites**
  (www.clarivate.com/products/incites).

InCites is a research evaluation tool, allowing the most comprehensive citation-based analysis of institutional research, based on the citation data of WoS. It is a

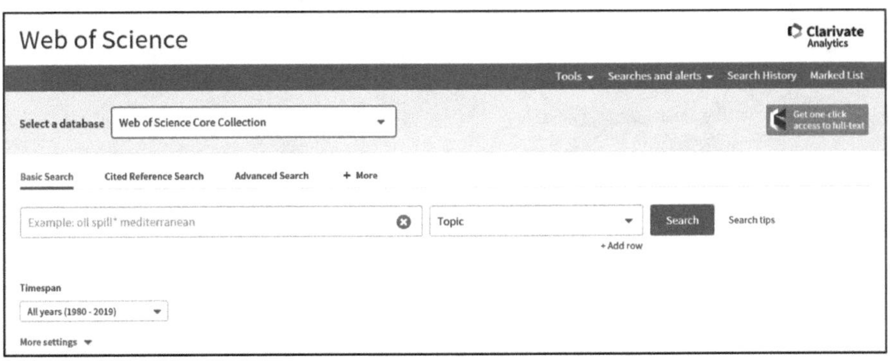

Fig. 8.17 Web of science search page (www.clarivate.com/products/web-of-science/databases)

A= total cites in 1992

B= 1992 cites to articles published in 1990-91 (this is a subset of A)

C= number of articles published in 1990-91

D= B/C = 1992 impact factor

Fig. 8.18 Calculation of journal citation impact. *Source* Clarivate Analytics https://clarivate.com/essays/impact-factor/

subscription service. The tool Essential Science Indicators (ESI), within InCites, highlights emerging science fronts as well as influential individuals, institutions, papers, journals, and countries in certain fields of research.

For instance, you are able to find the Highly Cited Papers and Highly Cited Researchers on InCites Essential Science Indicators.

Highly Cited Papers

Selected from the most recent 10 years of data, Highly Cited Papers reflect the top 1% of papers by field and publication year. Highly Cited Papers help identify breakthrough research within a research field and are used within WoS to identify and refine the most influential research papers.

Highly Cited Researchers

Clarivate Analysis releases every year the world-class researchers selected for their exceptional research performance, which is demonstrated by production of multiple highly cited papers that rank in the top 1% by citations for field and year in the Web of Science (WoS) (Fig. 8.19).

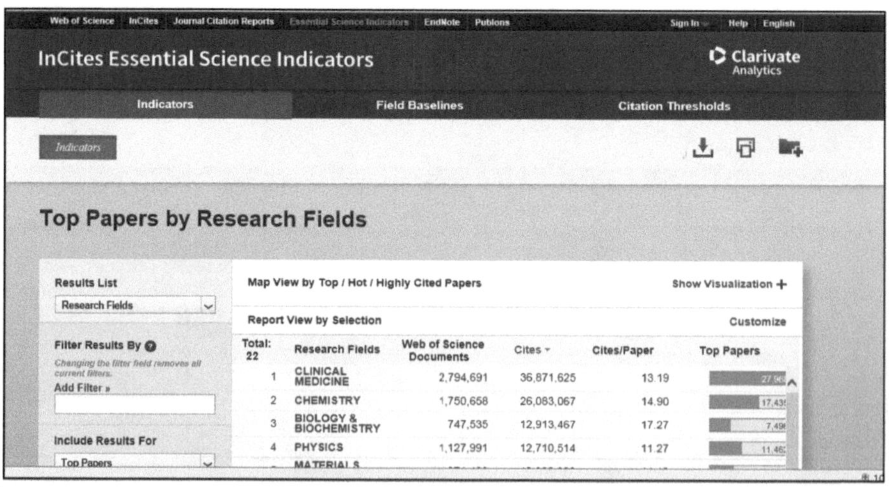

Fig. 8.19 InCites essential science indicators (hcr.clarivate.com)

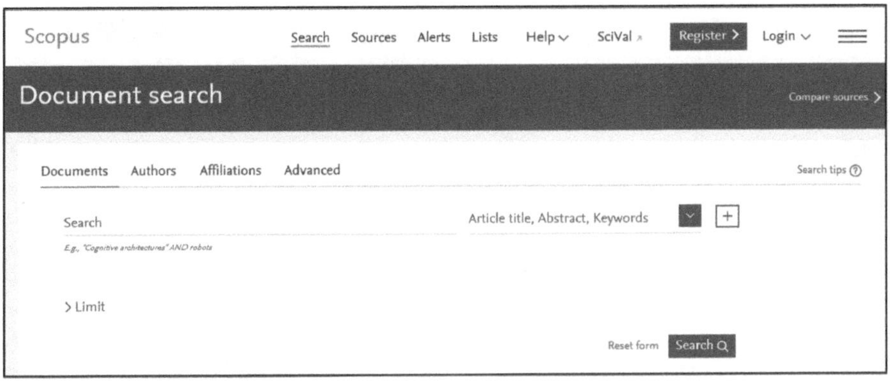

Fig. 8.20 Scopus search page (www.elsevier.com/solutions/scopus)

8.1.3.2 Scopus

Scopus, an Elsevier product, allows you to access a huge abstract and citation database of peer-reviewed literature. Just to give you an idea, it includes over 22,800 scientific journals, 150,000 books, 8 million conference papers from over 100,000 worldwide events, 39 million patent records, 16 million author profiles and much more (Fig. 8.20).

Scopus Author profiles can be searched freely online. It showcases various indicators. For a particular author, it is easy to locate number of citations, publication history and h-index (Fig. 8.21).[4]

SCImago Journal and Country Rank (SJR), a free website using the citation data of Scopus, exhibits the international academic journals and country ranking at https://www.scimagojr.com/. SJR was developed from the widely known algorithm Google PageRank[5] and thus takes into account of the importance and reputation of the citing journals or articles.

8.1.3.3 Google Scholar Citations

Google Scholar Citations provide a simple way for authors to create and keep track of citations to their articles. Use this free online tool and choose to have your list of articles updated automatically, review the updates yourself, or manually update your articles at any time (Fig. 8.22).

[4]h-index is an index intended to measure both the productivity and the impact of a particular scientist or scholar, or a group of scientists or scholars. For instance, a scientist has an index of h if h of his/her papers has at least h citations each (Source: www.blog.scopus.com).

[5]SCImago (n.d.). SJR—SCImago Journal and Country Rank. About Us. https://www.scimagojr.com/aboutus.php. Accessed January 15, 2019.

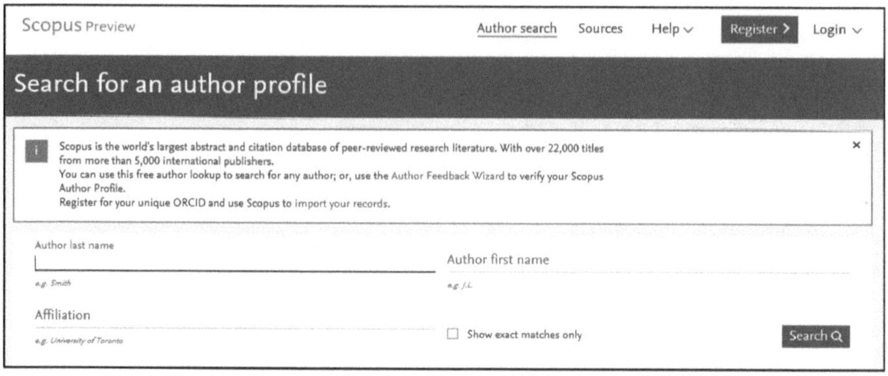

Fig. 8.21 Scopus author search (www.scopus.com/freelookup/form/author.uri)

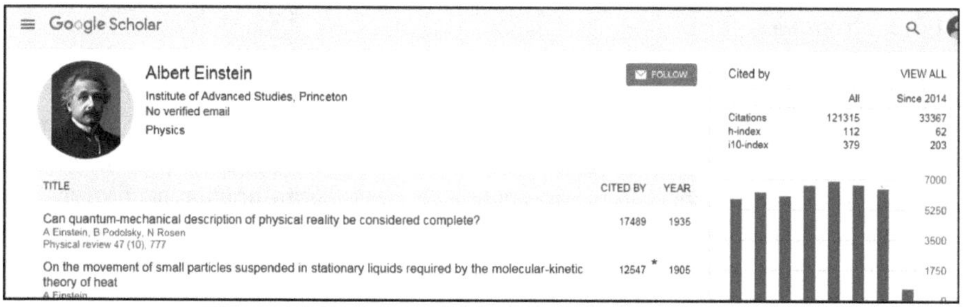

Fig. 8.22 Albert Einstein's Google Scholar citations (www.scholar.google.com)

8.1.3.4 Other Citation Analysis Tools

(1) Citation Analysis Tools in Particular Languages

The abovementioned citation analysis tools are from an international perspective and mainly for publications in English language, although they also cover other languages but not many. The following lists tools for some other languages.

- Chinese Social Sciences Citation Index (CSSCI)
  http://cssci.nju.edu.cn/ (Paid service)
- Chinese Science Citation Database (CSCD)
  http://sciencechina.cn/ (Paid service)
- A Guide to the Core Journals of China 中文核心期刊要目總覽
  (Released every 3 years in printed format only)
- Taiwan Social Sciences Citation Index (TSSCI)
  http://www.hss.ntu.edu.tw/model.aspx?no=67 (Free)

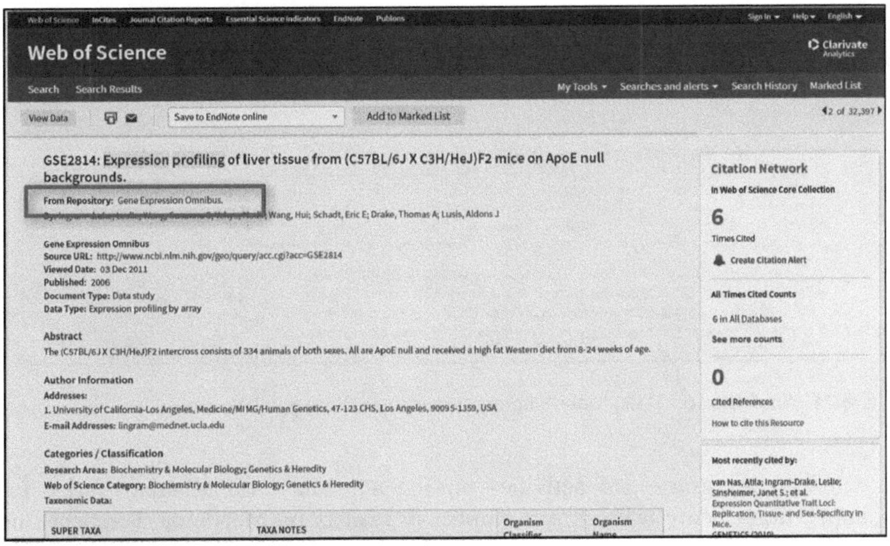

Fig. 8.23 Data citation index record on web of science (www.clarivate.com/products/web-of-science/web-science-form/data-citation-index/)

- Taiwan Citation Index—Humanities and Social Sciences (TCI-HSS)
  http://tci.ncl.edu.tw/ (Free)
- KCI-Korean Journal Database
  http://wokinfo.com/products_tools/multidisciplinary/kci_kjd/ (Paid service)
- Russian Science Citation Index
  http://wokinfo.com/products_tools/multidisciplinary/rsci/ (Paid service)
- SciELO Citation Index: for research in Latin America, Spain, Portugal, the Caribbean and South Africa
  http://wokinfo.com/products_tools/multidisciplinary/scielo/ (Paid service).

(2) **Data Citation Index (DCI)**

Data Citation Index (DCI), integrated on Web of Science platform, provides access to quality research data from about 400 strictly selected repositories[6] across disciplines and worldwide. This citation index intends to provide a clearer picture of full impact of research output, as well as to satisfy the needs for discoverability and citation standards for citing datasets (Fig. 8.23).

(3) **Altmetrics**

(www.altmetric.com/)

Altmetrics are non-traditional bibliometrics proposed as an alternative or complement to more traditional citation metrics such as Impact Factor or h-index.

[6]Master Data Repository List of DCI at http://wokinfo.com/products_tools/multidisciplinary/dci/repositories/search/.

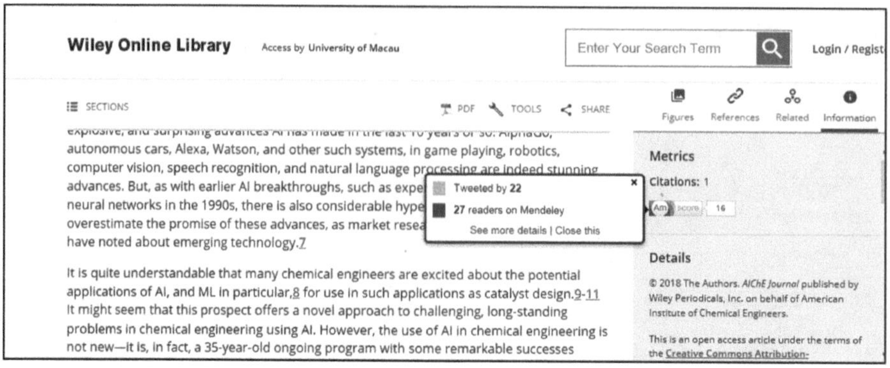

Fig. 8.24 Altmetrics on Wiley online library (www.onlinelibrary.wiley.com)

It demonstrates usage and activities on social media for particular works, for example, times being tweeted and number of readers on Mendeley. It reflects the social influence of a particular work (Fig. 8.24).

8.1.4 Bibliographic Management Tools

It is fundamental to do the citing when writing an academic work, which shows your respect of the intellectual property and avoids violating any copyright laws. However, to deal with all that bibliographic data and the reference materials are not easy jobs. Is there any way to manage bibliographic data and these important documents? The answer is yes. In this section, let's talk about some bibliographic management tools you can try.

- **EndNote**

EndNote is a reference management tool that assist you in collecting and curating the research materials and formatting bibliographies automatically. You can also get EndNote embedded in Word software so that you cite while you write. "Find Full Text" is great feature that help locate the full text of your stored bibliographic data online automatically. More, it further allows you to share bibliographic data with teammates. EndNote is a subscription service provided by Clarivate (Figs. 8.25 and 8.26).

- **RefWorks**

RefWorks is a reference management service with full-text management and collaboration features. It is a paid service provided by ProQuest (Fig. 8.27).

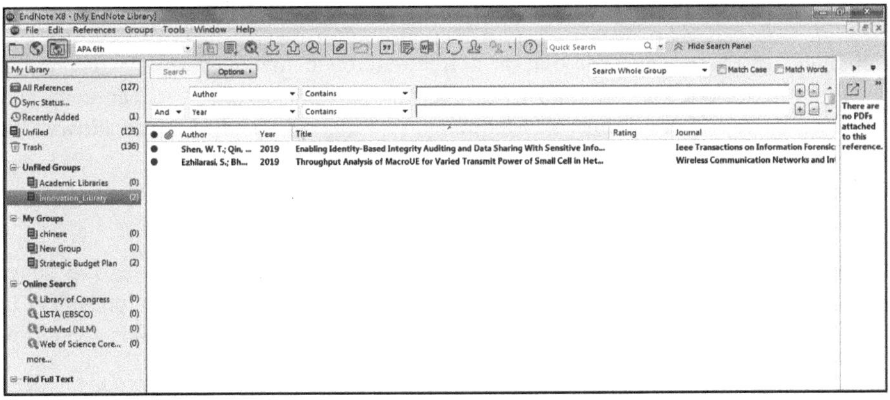

Fig. 8.25 EndNote X8 interface (www.endnote.com)

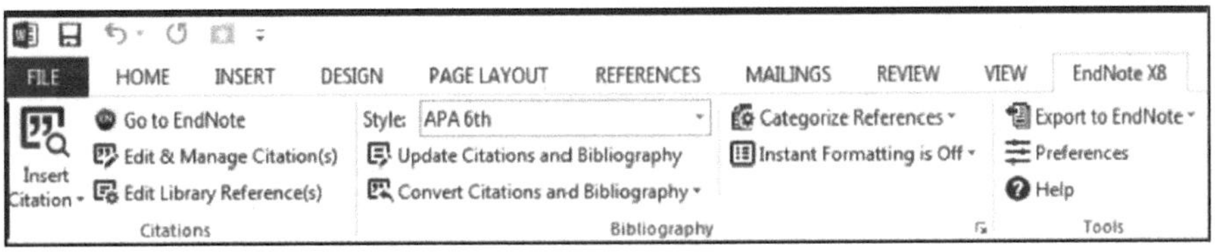

Fig. 8.26 EndNote X8 embedded in word (by the author)

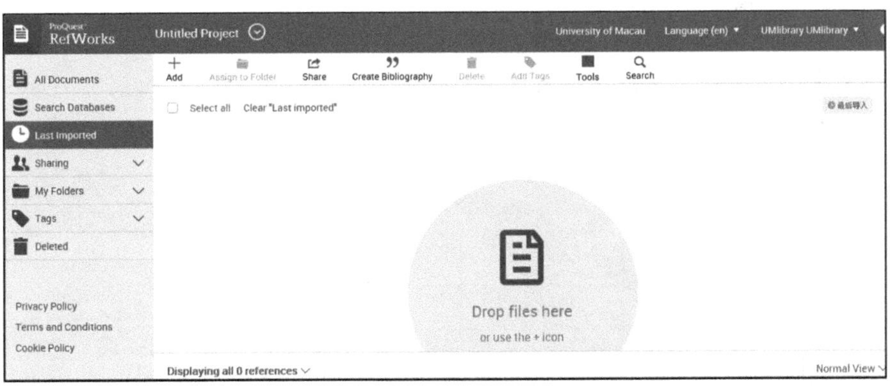

Fig. 8.27 RefWorks interface (www.proquest.com/products-services/refworks.html)

- **Mendeley**

Mendeley, produced by Elsevier, is a free reference manager and an academic social network. You can manage your research, showcase your work, connect and collaborate with others online on Mendeley. Its Citation Plugin feature allows you cite as you write with Word (Fig. 8.28).

- **Zotero**

Zotero is a free, easy-to-use tool to help you collect, organize, cite, and share research. You could save the research documents from online contents providers to Zotero directly in one step. Zotero toolbar could be installed in Word for citing when writing (Fig. 8.29).

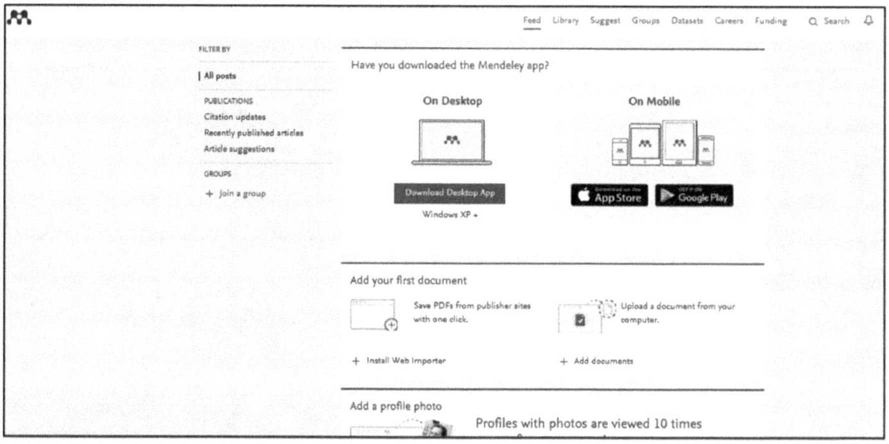

Fig. 8.28 Mendeley interface (www.mendeley.com)

Fig. 8.29 Zotero interface (www.zotero.org)

8.1.5 *Plagiarism and Similarity Checker*

Academic integrity requires that you give credit to authors and their ideas. Failure to do so is considered academic dishonesty. The International Center for Academic Integrity defines academic integrity as "a commitment, even in the face of adversity, to six fundamental values: honesty, trust, fairness, respect, responsibility, and courage."[7] In academic work, plagiarism is a dishonest behavior and should be avoided. University of Oxford states on its website that "plagiarism is presenting someone else's work or ideas as your own, with or without their consent, by incorporating it into your work without full acknowledgement."[8] Many professors ask you to use plagiarism and similarity checkers as you submit assignments for scoring. Most of these are commercial products and subscription-based.

- **Turnitin**
  (www.turnitin.com)

Turnitin allows you to view similarities of your work to the world's largest collection of Internet, academic, and student paper content. Instructors create courses and students submit their papers onto Turnitin for similarity checks. The matching text against Turnitin collection will be highlighted in the result report called "Originality Report". The Originality Report indicates the potential sources of plagiarism. High similarity percentage shown in the Originality Report may be considered plagiarism, depending on the status of the matching texts and the instructor's requirements of the student paper. Turnitin could be integrated with learning management systems such as Moodle and Blackboard so it is an easy part of the submission and assessment process (Fig. 8.30).

VeriGuide
VeriGuide is a plagiarism detection tool developed by the Chinese University of Hong Kong. It also allows the checking of the similarity of news articles on the Internet (Fig. 8.31).

8.2 Learning, Research and Collaboration

In this chapter, we have discussed five types of tools to support and enhance individual development of information literacy. These included (i) featured contents tools, (ii) online surveys and questionnaires, (iii) citation analysis tools, (iv) bibliographic management tools, and (v) plagiarism and text similarity checkers. We

---

[7]International Center for Academic Integrity (2017). Fundamental values of academic integrity. https://academicintegrity.org/fundamental-values/. Accessed January 28, 2019.

[8]University of Oxford (n.d.). Plagiarism. https://www.ox.ac.uk/students/academic/guidance/skills/plagiarism?wssl=1#. Accessed January 28, 2019.

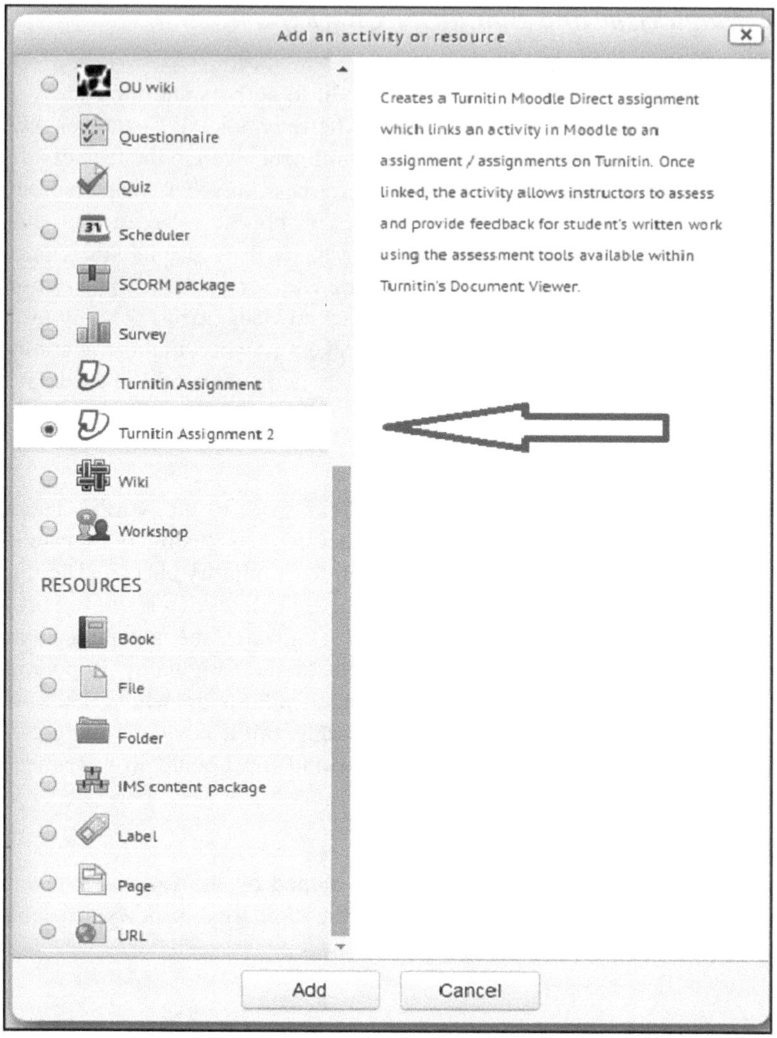

Fig. 8.30 Access Turnitin via Moodle (https://library.umac.mo/html/e_resources/turnitin_ummoodle_en.html)

discussed different kinds of featured contents tools used to discover information and verify sources. We learned tools for citation analysis, helping as we detect emerging research fronts and focus on important reading materials for a particular subjects or topics. Online survey and questionnaires tools encourage the implementation of sophisticated research, while bibliographic management tools assist in managing and organizing bibliographies and reference materials for citing and writing research papers. Plagiarism and similarity checkers are used widely in your academic work as safeguards of academic integrity and to help you avoid violating

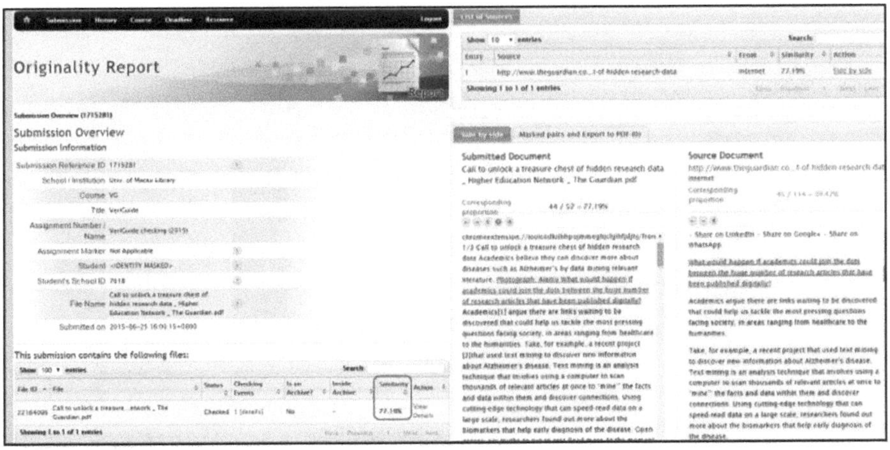

Fig. 8.31 Originality report of VeriGuide (www.veriguide.com)

copyright laws. We are fortunate to have access to so many high-quality resources and tools that support and enhance information literacy. Not only can we magnify the effectiveness of our own learning and research learning and research, but we can start to use online tools which enable sharing and collaborating among teammates both locally and world-wide.

Chapter 9
Assessment of Learning Outcomes for Information Literacy

Abstract This chapter discusses about the importance, process and methods of assessment for information literacy. It outlines the development of assessing information literacy from using standards to integrating framework into a learning environment.

9.1 Why Is the Assessment for Information Literacy Important?

Good assessment allows both students and teachers to improve in terms of recognized aspects found in assessment. Assessment is a process for quality improvement.

When teachers plan and design courses, learning objectives should be stated clearly so as to ensure that learning activities are relevant to course objectives. In this sense, standards are created to measure whether students have achieved the learning objectives. If they have, they should have gained expected knowledge or skills needed in upper level courses.

Information literacy is an ability to use information technology, to acquire information, to evaluate information and to use the knowledge gained in a person's study, work and everyday life. To understand if students have gained the ability of information literacy from certain courses or programs, assessment is needed.

9.2 Understanding Assessment Process of Information Literacy

Assessment is a process of quality improvement. To assess information literacy, how does the process of the assessment run? Saunders (2011, p. 156) described in her book *Information Literacy As a Student Learning Outcome* the assessment

B. T. H. Leung et al., *Transferring Information Literacy Practices*,
https://doi.org/10.1007/978-981-13-7743-3_9

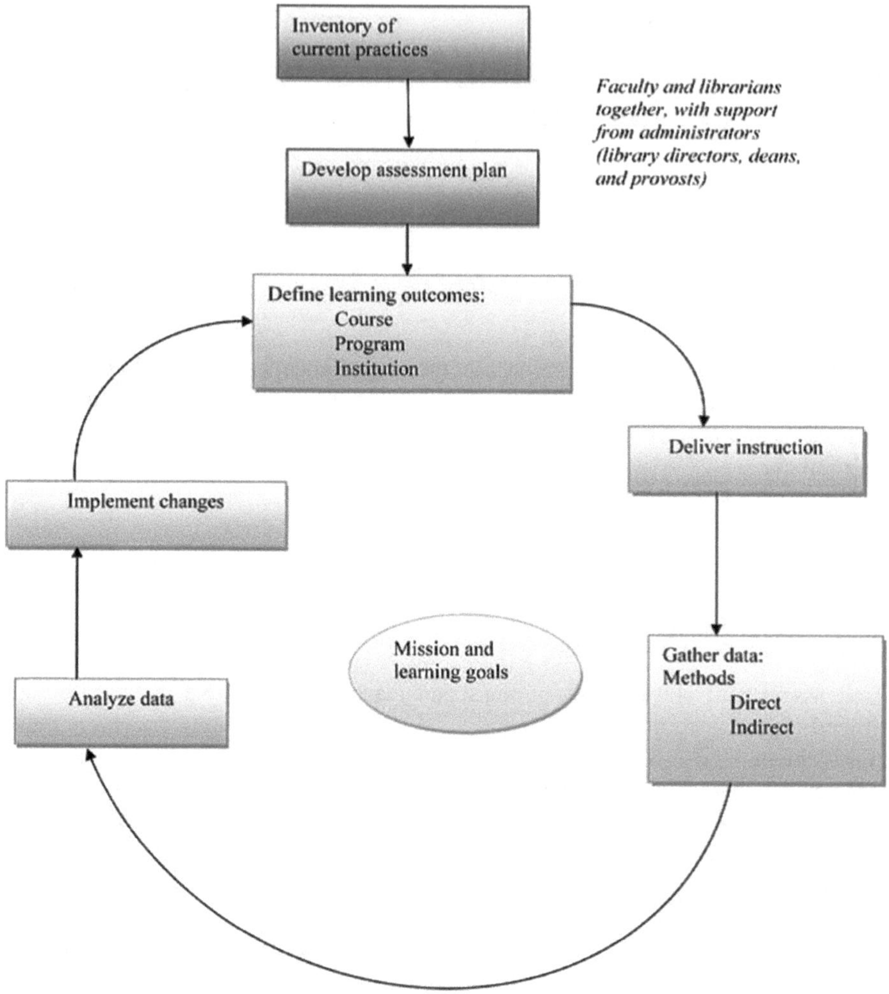

Fig. 9.1 Assessment process for information literacy (Saunders 2011)

process for information literacy in higher education (see Fig. 9.1): "Faculty and librarians review the current curriculum to identify areas where information literacy is addressed, and ensure that learning goals are explicitly defined at course, program, and institutional levels. Once they have identified the goals, faculty and librarians should engage in the iterative process of delivering instruction and gathering and analyzing evidence to determine where changes should be made." It was also emphasized that the mission and learning goals should be at the center of the assessment process and guide the relevant decisions.

9.3 ACRL Standards for Accessing Information Literacy

In 2000, *Information Literacy Competency Standards for Higher Education* was approved by the Association of College and Research Libraries (ACRL 2000). They provide a framework for assessing the information literate individual in higher education at all levels. Faculty and librarians should continue to work together to develop assessment instruments and strategies for particular disciplines. In this assessment of information literacy, there are 5 standards and 22 performance indicators provided (see Table 9.1). Accompanying outcomes for the corresponding standards are also indicated.

Table 9.1 ACRL information literacy competency standards for higher education

Standard One The Information literate student determines the nature and extent of the information needed **Performance Indicators** 1. The information literate student defines and articulates the need for information 2. The information literate student identifies a variety of types and formats of potential sources for information 3. The information literate student considers the costs and benefits of acquiring the needed information 4. The information literate student reevaluates the nature and extent of the information need
Standard Two The information literate student accesses needed information effectively and efficiently **Performance Indicators** 1. The information literate student selects the most appropriate investigative meth-ods or information retrieval systems for accessing the needed information 2. The information literate student constructs and implements effectively-designed search strategies 3. The information literate student retrieves information online or in person using a variety of methods 4. The information literate student refines the search strategy if necessary 5. The information literate student extracts, records, and manages the information and its sources
Standard Three The information literate student evaluates information and its sources critically and incorporates selected information into his or her knowledge base and value system **Performance Indicators** 1. The information literate student summarizes the main ideas to be extracted from the information gathered 2. The information literate student articulates and applies initial criteria for evaluating both the information and its sources 3. The information literate student synthesizes main ideas to construct new concepts 4. The information literate student compares new knowledge with prior knowledge to determine the value added, contradictions, or other unique characteristics of the information 5. The information literate student determines whether the new knowl-edge has an impact on the individual's value system and takes steps to reconcile differences

(continued)

Table 9.1 (continued)

6. The information literate student validates understanding and inter-pretation of the information through discourse with other individuals, subject-area experts, and/or practitioners 7. The information literate student determines whether the initial query should be revised
Standard Four The information literate student, individually or as a member of a group, uses information effectively to accomplish a specific purpose **Performance Indicators** 1. The information literate student applies new and prior information to the planning and creation of a particular product or performance 2. The information literate student revises the development process for the product or performance 3. The information literate student communicates the product or perfor-mance effectively to others
Standard Five The information literate student understands many of the economic, legal, and social issues surrounding the use of information and accesses and uses information ethically and legally **Performance Indicators** 1. The information literate student understands many of the ethical, legal and socio-economic issues surrounding information and information technology 2. The information literate student follows laws, regulations, institutional policies, and etiquette related to the access and use of information resources 3. The information literate student acknowledges the use of information sources in communicating the product or performance

After the release of the above ACRL Standards in 2000, many other standards and relevant documents were developed and put into practice around the world and across various disciplines. A few samples follow: *Information Literacy Standards for Science and Technology* (June 2006), *Information Literacy Standards for Anthropology and Sociology Students* (January 2008), *Political Science Research Competency Guidelines* (July 2008), *Psychology Information Literacy Standards* (June 2010), *Information Literacy Standards for Teacher Education* (May 2011), *Standards for Journalism Students and Professionals* (October 2011), *Visual Literacy Competency Standards for Higher Education* (October 2011), and *Information Literacy Competency Standards for Nursing* (October 2013).[1] Selected relevant standards and documents are listed in Appendix B.

ACRL *Information Literacy Competency Standards for Higher Education* were rescinded by the ACRL Board of Directors in 2016 and replaced by the new *Framework for Information Literacy for Higher Education*. In the coming section, we will discuss and see how the new framework works as the process of learning and engagement with core concepts.

[1]American Library Association. ACRL Standards, Guidelines, and Frameworks. http://www.ala.org/acrl/standards/standardsguidelinestopic. Accessed February 15, 2019.

9.4 Assessment Methods and Instruments for Information Literacy

9.4.1 Assessment Methods

> It is crucial to use a multimethod and multisource approach to assessment in order to obtain maximum validity and to reduce potential error or bias associated with any one approach (Prus and Johnson 1994).

Prus and Johnson 1994 discussed the assessment methods and the relative advantages and disadvantages. Those methods are summarized briefly below.

- Tests: standardized, locally developed and oral;
- Competency-Based methods: performance appraisals, simulations, and others;
- Self-Report and third-part reports: surveys, exit interviews, reports from employers, etc.;
- Behavioral observations;
- Portfolios of student work: these can include papers, assignments, etc.

Other methods of assessment that can be used to determine student outcomes in the context of information literacy include active course-learning techniques, audiovisual aids, collaborative learning exercises, debates, focused library activities, and more (Neely 2006, p. 7). Walsh (2009) reviewed 127 relevant academic articles and categorized them into 9 types of information literacy assessment methods, namely, analysis of bibliographies, essay, final grades, multiple choice questionnaire, observation, portfolio, quiz/text, self-assessment and simulation. The most popular one is multiple choice questionnaire.

If these information literacy skills have not traditionally been taught, it will be interesting to see how, how often and at what points they might be assessed in a university program that is starting to teach them. We believe that results will allow clearer insight into the learning process as information literacy skills are encouraged and essential nowadays.

9.4.2 Assessment Instruments

Sample surveys and instruments for assessment information literacy from all over the world have been designed based on existing assessment standards and documents. 3 popular pre-developed instruments are introduced below.

- Tool for Real-Time Assessment of Information Literacy Skills (TRAILS) http://www.trails-9.org/howTrailsWorks2.php?page=works.

TRAILS, a project of Kent State University Libraries, is a knowledge assessment with multiple-choice questions targeting a variety of information literacy skills based on 3rd, 6th, 9th, and 12th grade standards. The assessment items are based on the *American Association of School Librarians' Standards for the 21st-Century Learner*[2] and the *Common Core State Standards Initiative*. It is available online free of charge.

- Standardized Assessment of Information Literacy Skills (SAILS) https://www.projectsails.org/site/the-test/.

SAILS, a commercial pre-developed test, is a nationally-recognized assessment of information literacy skills. There are three forms for this instrument: one gives individual test results, one is for groups (cohorts) of students, and one allows you to select the test questions. All these tests are based on the *ACRL Information Literacy Competency Standards for Higher Education*.

- Research Readiness Self-Assessment (RRSA) https://scholarly.cmich.edu/?a=d&d=CMUOther2008-01.1.1&.

RRSA, an interactive online assessment and feedback application designed by Central Michigan University. It is a paid instrument. It measures information age competencies: basic and advanced search skills, understanding of scholarly resources, critical judgment of secondary source information, understanding of plagiarism and others.

Those instruments are mainly based on Western norms, for English-speaking countries or for learners studying or taught in English. To apply them to non-English context, the effects of socio-cultural factors should be considered (Hani Syazillah et al. 2018). Appendix C lists some more selected and valuable instruments, commercial or free, pre-developed or customized, for assessment of information literacy around the world.

9.5 Framework for Information Literacy for Higher Education

The standard approach to information literacy has been criticized by some as too prescriptive and not reflective of changes in the higher education environment and in the production and dissemination of information in the 21st century. In 2011, a task force for revising the ACRL Standards for information literacy came into existence. The new *Framework for Information Literacy for Higher Education* emerged (Gersch et al. 2016) and was adopted by ACRL in 2016. The new Framework "places greater emphasis on student engagement with core concepts, and on questioning, collaboration, and conversation than the more discretely

[2]It was replaced by *AASL Standards Framework for Learners* in 2018.

defined Standards did" (Anderson 2015). "Perhaps the single-largest difference between the previous set of ACRL information literacy guidelines and the proposed framework is the transition from a skill-based focus to one of knowledge-based learning and discovery" (Knapp and Brower 2014, p. 466). The newer framework document (ACRL 2015) is based on a cluster of interconnected core concepts with flexible options for implementation. Six core concepts are linked to sets of knowledge practices (demonstrations of ways in which learners can increase their understanding of information literacy concepts), and a set of dispositions (ways to address the affective, attitudinal, or valuing dimensions of learning). Each library and its partners on campus, i.e. faculty and administrators, will need to deploy these frames to best fit their own situation, including designing learning outcomes. The six core concepts, with no particular sequence in which they must be learned, are:

1. **Authority Is Constructed and Contextual**
   Information resources reflect their creators' expertise and credibility, and are evaluated based on the information need and the context in which the information will be used. Authority is constructed in that various communities may recognize different types of authority. It is contextual in that the information need may help to determine the level of authority required.
2. **Information Creation as a Process**
   Information in any format is produced to convey a message and is shared via a selected delivery method. The iterative processes of researching, creating, revising, and disseminating information vary, and the resulting product reflects these differences.
3. **Information has Value**
   Information possesses several dimensions of value, including as a commodity, as a means of education, as a means to influence, and as a means of negotiating and understanding the world. Legal and socioeconomic interests influence information production and dissemination.
4. **Research as Inquiry**
   Research is iterative and depends upon asking increasingly complex or new questions whose answers in turn develop additional questions or lines of inquiry in any field.
5. **Scholarship as Conversation**
   Communities of scholars, researchers, or professionals engage in sustained discourse with new insights and discoveries occurring over time as a result of varied perspectives and interpretations.
6. **Searching as Strategic Exploration**
   Searching for information is often nonlinear and iterative, requiring the evaluation of a range of information sources and the mental flexibility to pursue alternate avenues as new understanding develops.

Using this framework, information literacy is viewed as an overarching set of abilities, a “metaliteracy”, which demands behavioral, affective, cognitive, and metacognitive engagement with the information ecosystem. This concept offers a renewed vision of in which students are consumers and creators of information who can participate successfully in collaborative spaces.

Recent research has been emphasizing on metaliteracy and its integration or collaboration with normal courses in various subjects. Metaliteracy is not a thing separated from the regular courses but a set of abilities wedged in the information ecosystem of a variety of subject learning and coursework.

References

Anderson MJ (2015) Rethinking assessment: information literacy instruction and the ACRL framework. SLIS Stud Res J 5(2). http://scholarworks.sjsu.edu/slissrj/vol5/iss2/3

Association of College and Research Libraries (2000) Information literacy competency standards for higher education. http://www.ala.org/acrl/standards/informationliteracycompetency

Association of College and Research Libraries (2015) Framework for information literacy for higher education. http://www.ala.org/acrl/sites/ala.org.acrl/files/content/issues/infolit/Framework_ILHE.pdf

Banta TW et al (1996) Assessment in practice: putting principles to work on college campuses. Jossey-Bass, San Francisco

Gersch B, Lampner W, Turner D (2016) Collaborative metaliteracy: putting the new information literacy framework into (digital) practice. J Libr Inf Serv Distance Learn 10(3–4):199–214. https://doi.org/10.1080/1533290X.2016.1206788

Hani Syazillah N, Kiran K, Chowdhury G (2018) Adaptation, translation, and validation of information literacy assessment instrument. J Assoc Inf Sci Technol 69:996–1006. https://doi.org/10.1002/asi.24023

Hutchings P, Ewell P, Banta T (2012) AAHE principles of good practice. National Institute for Learning Outcomes Assessment. http://learningoutcomesassessment.org/PrinciplesofAssessment.html. Accessed 15 Feb 2019

Knapp M, Brower S (2014) The ACRL framework for information literacy in higher education: implications for health sciences librarianship. Med Ref Ser Q 33(4):460–468

Mackey TP, Jacobson TE (2011) Reframing information literacy as a metaliteracy. Coll Res Libr 72(1):62–78

Neely TY (2006) Information literacy assessment: standards-based tools and assignments. Am Libr Assoc, Chicago

Pausch LM, Popp MP (2006) Assessment of information literacy: lessons from the higher education assessment movement. American Library Association. http://www.ala.org/acrl/publications/whitepapers/nashville/pauschpopp. Accessed 15 Feb 2019

Prus J, Johnson (1994). A critical review of student assessment options. New Directions for Community Colleges, no. 88 (Winter 1994), pp 69–83

Saunders L (2011) Information literacy as a student learning outcome: the perspective of institutional accreditation, ABC-CLIO, LLC. From ProQuest Ebook Central. https://ebookcentral-proquest-com.libezproxy.umac.mo/lib/umac/detail.action?docID=871477. Accessed 15 Feb 2019

Walsh A (2009) Information literacy assessment: where do we start? J Librariansh Inf Sci 41 (1):19–28. https://doi.org/10.1177/0961000608099896

Appendix A
Online Tutorials for Information Literacy Tools

1. Google Forms: GSuite
   https://gsuite.google.com/learning-center/products/forms/get-started/#!/
2. Survey Monkey
   https://help.surveymonkey.com/categories/Design_Manage
3. Qualtrics
   https://www.qualtrics.com/support/survey-platform/getting-started/survey-platform-overview/
4. Web of Science
   http://clarivate.libguides.com/home
5. Scopus
   https://service.elsevier.com/app/overview/scopus/
6. Data Citation Index
   https://clarivate.libguides.com/webofscienceplatform/dci
7. Altmetrics
   https://www.altmetric.com/about-altmetrics/what-are-altmetrics/
8. EndNote
   http://clarivate.libguides.com/endnote_training/home
9. Refworks
   https://www.refworks.com/tutorial/
10. Mendeley
    https://www.mendeley.com/guides/videos
11. Zotero
    https://www.zotero.org/support/screencast_tutorials
12. Turnitin
    https://guides.turnitin.com/01_Manuals_and_Guides
13. Veriguide
    https://veriguide1.cse.cuhk.edu.hk/portal/plagiarism_detection/manuals.jsp.

B. T. H. Leung et al., *Transferring Information Literacy Practices*,
https://doi.org/10.1007/978-981-13-7743-3

Appendix B
Standards and Documents for Assessing Information Literacy

1. Objectives for Information Literacy Instruction: A Model Statement for Academic Librarians (Released January 2001). http://www.ala.org/acrl/standards/objectivesinformation
2. Australian and New Zealand Information Literacy Framework: principles, standards and practice (Released 2004). http://archive.caul.edu.au/info-literacy/InfoLiteracyFramework.pdf
3. Information Literacy Standards for Science and Technology (Released June 2006). http://www.ala.org/acrl/standards/infolitscitech
4. Research Competency Guidelines for Literatures in English (Released June 2007). http://www.ala.org/acrl/standards/researchcompetenciesles
5. Information Literacy Standards for Anthropology and Sociology Students (Released January 2008). http://www.ala.org/acrl/standards/anthro_soc_standards
6. Political Science Research Competency Guidelines (Released July 2008). http://www.ala.org/acrl/sites/ala.org.acrl/files/content/standards/PoliSciGuide.pdf
7. Psychology Information Literacy Standards (Released June 2010). http://www.ala.org/acrl/standards/psych_info_lit
8. Common Core State Standards Initiative (Released 2010). http://www.corestandards.org/read-the-standards/
9. The SCONUL Seven Pillars of Information Literacy Core Model for Higher Education (Released April 2011). https://www.sconul.ac.uk/sites/default/files/documents/coremodel.pdf
10. Information Literacy Standards for Teacher Education (Released May 2011). http://www.ala.org/acrl/sites/ala.org.acrl/files/content/standards/ilstandards_te.pdf
11. Information Literacy Competency Standards for Journalism Students and Professionals (Released October 2011). http://www.ala.org/acrl/sites/ala.org.acrl/files/content/standards/il_journalism.pdf
12. Visual Literacy Competency Standards for Higher Education (Released October 2011). http://www.ala.org/acrl/standards/visualliteracy
13. Guidelines for Instruction Programs in Academic Libraries (Released October 2011). http://www.ala.org/acrl/standards/guidelinesinstruction

B. T. H. Leung et al., *Transferring Information Literacy Practices*,
https://doi.org/10.1007/978-981-13-7743-3

14. Information Literacy Framework for Wales (Released 2011). https://libraries.wales/wp-content/uploads/2016/06/Information_Literacy_Framework_Wales.pdf
15. Information Literacy Competency Standards for Nursing (Released October 2013). http://www.ala.org/acrl/standards/visualliteracy
16. Framework for Information Literacy in Higher Education (Released February 2015, January 2016). http://www.ala.org/acrl/standards/ilframework
17. Information Literacy for Hong Kong Students (Released May 2018). https://www.edb.gov.hk/attachment/en/edu-system/primary-secondary/applicable-to-primary-secondary/it-in-edu/Information-Literacy/IL20180516E.pdf
18. AASL Standards Framework for Learners (Released 2018). https://standards.aasl.org/framework/
19. Characteristics of Programs of Information Literacy that Illustrate Best Practices: A Guideline (January Released 2019). http://www.ala.org/acrl/standards/characteristics.

Appendix C
Selected Instruments for Assessment of Information Literacy

1. Tool for Real-Time Assessment of Information Literacy Skills (TRAILS) by Kent State University Libraries. http://www.trails-9.org/howTrailsWorks2.php?page=works
2. Standardized Assessment of Information Literacy Skills (SAILS) by Kent State University. https://www.projectsails.org/site/the-test/
3. Research Readiness Self-Assessment (RRSA) by Central Michigan University. https://scholarly.cmich.edu/?a=d&d=CMUOther2008-01.1.1&
4. Information Literacy Test (ILT) by James Madison University. https://www.madisonassessment.com/assessment-testing/information-literacy-test/
5. iSkills by Educational Testing Service (ETS). https://doi.org/10.1002/ets2.12211
6. Threshold Achievement Test for Information Literacy (TATIL) from Carrick Enterprises. https://thresholdachievement.com/field-test-information
7. HEDS Research Practices Survey by Higher Education Data Sharing Consortium. https://www.hedsconsortium.org/heds-research-practices-survey/
8. Standard's Key to Information Literacy. http://skil.stanford.edu/sitemap/index.html
9. Information Literacy Assessment by Madonna University. http://library.madonna.edu/information-literacy/
10. Information Literacy Assessment by the University of Akron Wayne College Library. http://libguides.uakron.edu/wayne_InformationLiteracy/assessment
11. Madison Research Essential Skills Test (MREST) by James Madison University. https://www.jmu.edu/gened/MREST.shtml.

B. T. H. Leung et al., *Transferring Information Literacy Practices*,
https://doi.org/10.1007/978-981-13-7743-3

Index

B. T. H. Leung et al., *Transferring Information Literacy Practices*,
https://doi.org/10.1007/978-981-13-7743-3

FSC
www.fsc.org
MIX
Papier | Fördert gute Waldnutzung
FSC® C083411

Kolibri 360 GmbH
Ferdinand-Jühlke-Straße 7
99095 Erfurt, Deutschland
produktsicherheit@kolibri360.de